First World War
and Army of Occupation
War Diary
France, Belgium and Germany

32 DIVISION
Divisional Troops
B Squadron South Irish Horse
5 August 1914 - 31 May 1916

WO95/2380/1

Published by

The Naval & Military Press Ltd

Unit 10 Ridgewood Industrial Park,

Uckfield, East Sussex,

TN22 5QE England

Tel: +44 (0) 1825 749494

www.naval-military-press.com

www.nmarchive.com

This diary has been reprinted in facsimile from the original. Any imperfections are inevitably reproduced and the quality may fall short of modern type and cartographic standards.

© **Crown Copyright**
Images reproduced by permission of The National Archives, London, England, 2015.

Contents

Document type	Place/Title	Date From	Date To
Heading	WO95/2380 (1)		
Heading	32 Div Troops "B" Sqn Stn Irish Horse 1914 Aug-1916 May. To 15 Corrs.		
Heading	I Corps Cavalry Disembarked Le Havre 19.8.14. "B" Squadron South Irish Horse August To December 1914		
War Diary	Dublin.	05/08/1914	18/08/1914
War Diary	Le Havre	19/08/1914	21/08/1914
War Diary	Bussigny	22/08/1914	23/08/1914
War Diary	Bavai.	24/08/1914	24/08/1914
War Diary	Landrecies.	25/08/1914	25/08/1914
War Diary	Jerusalem	26/08/1914	26/08/1914
War Diary	Origny	27/08/1914	27/08/1914
War Diary	Gotain.	28/08/1914	29/08/1914
War Diary	Foissons	30/08/1914	30/08/1914
War Diary	Villiers Cotterets	31/08/1914	31/08/1914
War Diary	Meaux	01/09/1914	02/09/1914
War Diary	Goiron	03/09/1914	03/09/1914
War Diary	Gauard Signy	04/09/1914	04/09/1914
War Diary	Chaumes.	05/09/1914	05/09/1914
War Diary	Chateau Charboisson.	06/09/1914	06/09/1914
War Diary	Choisy.	07/09/1914	07/09/1914
War Diary	Rebais.	08/09/1914	08/09/1914
War Diary	Chaolyo-Sur-Morne.	09/09/1914	09/09/1914
War Diary	Hauteuesnes.	10/09/1914	10/09/1914
War Diary	Dalchy Breny.	11/09/1914	11/09/1914
War Diary	Gouignes	12/09/1914	12/09/1914
War Diary	Courcelles.	13/09/1914	14/09/1914
War Diary	Dhuizel	15/09/1914	28/09/1914
War Diary	Courcelles.	29/09/1914	03/10/1914
War Diary	Belcher	04/10/1914	14/10/1914
War Diary	Braine.	15/10/1914	15/10/1914
War Diary	Fene-En-Tardemois	16/10/1914	17/10/1914
War Diary	St. Omer	18/10/1914	18/10/1914
War Diary	Cassel	19/10/1914	19/10/1914
War Diary	Poperinghe	20/10/1914	20/10/1914
War Diary	Ypres.	21/10/1914	04/11/1914
War Diary	Elverdinge.	05/11/1914	21/11/1914
War Diary	Hazebrouck.	22/11/1914	22/12/1914
War Diary	Hinges.	23/12/1914	31/12/1914
Heading	B Squadron (2Troops) S. Irish Horse. Capt Troops IV Corps Vol I December 1914 To January 1915		
Miscellaneous	War Diary Detachment South Irish Horse (2 Troops) Attached H.Q. 4 Th Corps.		
Miscellaneous	Princess Mary's Gifts.		
Miscellaneous		31/01/1915	31/01/1915
Miscellaneous	Princess Mary's Gifts.		
Heading	32nd Div "B" Sq. S. Irish Horse Vol I		
War Diary	Havre	25/11/1915	25/11/1915
War Diary	Pont Remy	26/11/1915	26/11/1915
War Diary	Famechon	28/11/1915	29/11/1915

War Diary	Flesselles	01/12/1915	07/12/1915
War Diary	Behencourt	20/12/1915	30/12/1915
War Diary	Le Quesnoy	01/12/1915	29/12/1915
War Diary	Beaurepaire (Lillers)	30/12/1915	31/12/1915
Heading	B Squad S.Irish Horse 32nd Div Vol 3		
Miscellaneous	O.C. B. Squadron South Irish Horse (32nd Div Cavalry) D.A.G. G.H.Q. 3rd Echelon.		
War Diary	Havre	25/11/1915	25/11/1915
War Diary	Pont Remy	26/11/1915	26/11/1915
War Diary	Famechon	28/11/1915	29/11/1915
War Diary	Flesselles	01/12/1915	07/12/1915
War Diary	Behencourt	20/12/1915	29/01/1916
Heading	32nd Divisional Cavalry "B" Squadron South Irish Horse January 1916		
War Diary	Behencourt	01/01/1916	29/01/1916
Heading	32nd Divisional Cavalry "B" Squadron South Irish Horse February 1916		
War Diary	Behencourt	01/02/1916	21/02/1916
Heading	32nd Divisional Cavalry "B" Squadron South Irish Horse March 1916		
War Diary	Behencourt	01/03/1916	31/03/1916
Heading	32nd Divisional Cavalry "B" Squadron South Irish Horse April 1916		
War Diary	Behencourt	01/04/1916	30/04/1916
Heading	32nd Divisional Cavalry Became XVth Corps Cavalry 14.5.16. "B" Squadron South Irish Horse May 1916		
War Diary	Contay	01/05/1916	14/05/1916
War Diary	Heilly	17/05/1916	31/05/1916

MBA/2380/(1)

MBA/2380/(1)

~~32ND DIVISION~~
~~DIVL TROOPS~~ TROOPS

32 DIV TROOPS

'B' SQN 5TH IRISH HORSE

1914 AUG — 1916 MAY

TO 15 CORPS

2168

I CORPS CAVALRY

Disembarked LE HAVRE 19.8.14.

"B" SQUADRON

SOUTH IRISH HORSE

AUGUST TO DECEMBER 1914.

Army Form C. 2118.

WAR DIARY
or
INTELLIGENCE SUMMARY.
(Erase heading not required.)

Instructions regarding War Diaries and Intelligence Summaries are contained in F. S. Regs., Part II. and the Staff Manual respectively. Title pages will be prepared in manuscript.

Hour, Date, Place	Summary of Events and Information	Remarks and references to Appendices
1914 August 5. Dublin.	Mobilize	
" 6	2nd day of mobilization	
" 7	3rd " " "	
" 8	4th " " "	
" 9	5th " " "	
" 10	6th " " "	
" 11	7th " " "	
" 12	8th " " "	
" 13	9th " " "	
" 14	10th " " "	
" 15	11th " " "	
" 16	12th " " "	
" 17	Embarked at Alexandra Basin	
" 18	At Sea	
" 19 Le Havre	Landed at Le Havre	
" 20 "	Rest Camp	
" 21 "	Entrain & proceed to Landrecies destination	
" 22 Busigny	Bivouac at Beaufort	
" 23 "	Continue march & join 10th Inf. Brigade at Bavencourt. Draw stores MABUGE	
" 24 Boyrey	Bivouac at Vieux Mesnil	
" 25 Landrecies	Heavy attack from 2.30 PM till 9.30. When stormed in Action	
" 26 Gussalan Leen	Sent out to the Front Just stand Reserve in battle of Le Cateau	
" 27 Origny	On the up Retrement Start, Remained Rd & Guard	

Army Form C. 2118.

WAR DIARY
or
INTELLIGENCE SUMMARY.
(Erase heading not required.)

Instructions regarding War Diaries and Intelligence Summaries are contained in F. S. Regs., Part II. and the Staff Manual respectively. Title pages will be prepared in manuscript.

Hour, Date, Place	Summary of Events and Information	Remarks and references to Appendices
1914 August 28 St. Quentin	Halted	
" 29 "	"	
" 30 Soissons	Sent to Contact Sqn. & went to Vereuil. Met Germans at Mantes. Germans entering Mongst killed at ind French attack.	
" 31 Villiers Cotterets	"	
September 1 Meaux	Germans Shorn as Cavalry on the Front of the above in reen.	
" 2 "	Night march	
" 3 Going further		
" 4 Favards Sgnts Sigh H.		
" 5 St Vaury	Sent to MacPherson to the base that I was from the North of S. MacPherson.	
" 6 St Jean Weptraine		
" 7 Vinjoy		
" 8 Pipers		
" 9 Chezy-en-Orxan	A.D. V. Insp Came to G.H.Q.	
" 10 Fontenous	One troop sent with Stenniss to Red Head.	
" 11 Soulvigny	Received first mail at the Lennis home. Towards of rain all night.	
" 12 Longueu	Sent on to Sons at 1750 during the night letting the Sermens turning up somewhere. Bridge.	
" 13 Bonnelles	Sent to Borry at daybreak who in deforting is siege. CHAVONNE. Under heavy shell fire all day.	
" 14 "	Sent to BOURG. Under heavy shell fire all day. 3 horses hit.	
" 15 Chivijel	"	
" 16 "	"	
" 17 "	"	
" 18 "	"	
" 19 "	Out all night looking for the enemy spies in the troops town ALONGEVAL.	

Army Form C. 2118.

WAR DIARY
or
INTELLIGENCE SUMMARY.
(Erase heading not required.)

Instructions regarding War Diaries and Intelligence Summaries are contained in F. S. Regs., Part II. and the Staff Manual respectively. Title pages will be prepared in manuscript.

Hour, Date, Place	Summary of Events and Information	Remarks and references to Appendices
1914 September 20 Bluzy	Sent to rein force 2nd Cavalry Bde at CHAVONNE.	
" 21 "		
" 22 "		
" 23 "	[B sent to C in C 1st Infantry nbg.	
" 24 "		
" 25 "		
" 26 "	Searched woods near LONGEVAL	
" 27 "	Shelled at ½ Billets. 1 man hit 2 horses killed. 3 horses killed while in care billets it.	
" 28 "		
" 29 Courcelles		
" 30 "	Searched Woods in DHUZEL — BRAINE Wood.	
October 1 "	"	
" 2 "	"	
" 3 "		
" 4 Beheme		
" 5 "	Searched Woods around BRENELLES.	
" 6 "	"	
" 7 "	"	
" 8 "	"	
" 9 "		
" 10 "	Sent to CHESSIMY, searched Woods in conjunction with French Ter. & Sipper Regt. Shelled from PAILLY across the river while in place in search.	
" 11 "		
" 12 "		
" 13 "		
" 14 "		

Army Form C. 2118

WAR DIARY
or
INTELLIGENCE SUMMARY.
(Erase heading not required.)

Instructions regarding War Diaries and Intelligence Summaries are contained in F. S. Regs., Part II. and the Staff Manual respectively. Title pages will be prepared in manuscript.

Hour, Date, Place	Summary of Events and Information	Remarks and references to Appendices
1914 October 15 Boisne	March to Fives-en-Tardenois	
" 16 Fives-en-Tardenois	Tardenois Entrain at 2 am	
" 17	Detrain nr PARIS to St OMER.	
" 18 St Omer		
" 19 Cassel		
" 20 Poperinge		
" 21 Ypres.	Sent to assist G.O.C. 7th DIVISION at SANDVOORDA.	
" 22 "		
" 23 "	Sent to support CONNAUGHT RANGERS in wood nr MENIN ROAD.	
" 24 "		
" 25 "	Sent to support 3rd Cav. Bde at HOLLEBEKE, it there became till 26 inst.	
" 26 "		
" 27 "	In support of Cavalry Bde in MENIN WOOD. Shelled out of CHATEAU at HOOGE.	
" 29 "		
" 30 "	In support of 1st DIVISION at HOOGE. 1st Army attack of BAVARIANS	Squadron ordered to take the communication, this patrol is to which the 1st Corps & Cav. Division (see next page)
" 31 "	" 2nd "	
November 1 "	" "	
" 2 "		
" 3 "	Support Centre of YPRES Heavily shelled. 3 hrs & 3 hrs of Squadron hit.	
" 4 Flurdinghe	Support 1st Division at ZILLE BEKE. Sent to pick up communication	
" 5 "	with French who were very hard hit this.	
" 6 "		

Army Form C. 2118.

WAR DIARY
or
INTELLIGENCE SUMMARY.
(Erase heading not required.)

Hour, Date, Place	Summary of Events and Information	Remarks and references to Appendices
1912 November 7 Elverdinghe	Halted	During this time the Whole of the communications of the 1st Corps to Parish Sub station were carried out by the Section. The wires were to function from Div. Hd. gtrs to the two Divisions Hd. gtrs. & also from Hd. gtrs. at more than the 4th phone & telegraph wires were cut owing to visits of the enemy to a daily to shell fire.
" 8	"	
" 9	"	
" 10	"	
" 11	"	
" 12	"	
" 13	"	
" 14	"	
" 15	"	
" 16	"	
" 17	"	
" 18	"	
" 19	"	
" 20	"	
" 21	Leave Elverdinghe at 7 A.M. and arrive at Hazebrouck 4 pm	
" 22 Hazebrouck	1st Corps hd. drawn from the line is rested.	
" 23	"	
" 24	"	
" 25	"	
" 26	"	
" 27	"	
" 28	"	
" 29	"	
" 30	"	

Army Form C. 2118.

WAR DIARY
or
INTELLIGENCE SUMMARY.
(Erase heading not required.)

Instructions regarding War Diaries and Intelligence Summaries are contained in F.S. Regs., Part II. and the Staff Manual respectively. Title pages will be prepared in manuscript.

Hour, Date, Place	Summary of Events and Information	Remarks and references to Appendices
1914 December 1 Hazebrouck		
2 "		
3 "		
4 "		
5 "		
6 "		
7 "		
8 "		
9 "		
10 "		
11 "	That (who withdrew from the 2th inst)	
12 "		
13 "		
14 "		
15 "		
16 "		
17 "		
18 "		
19 "		
20 "		
21 "		
22 "		
23 Amiens		
24 "		
25 "	Left Hazebrouck at 5.30 a.m. & arrived at Amiens	
26 "		

Army Form C. 2118.

WAR DIARY
or
INTELLIGENCE SUMMARY
(Erase heading not required.)

Instructions regarding War Diaries and Intelligence Summaries are contained in F. S. Regs., Part II. and the Staff Manual respectively. Title pages will be prepared in manuscript.

Hour, Date, Place	Summary of Events and Information	Remarks and References to Appendices
1942. December 27 Knight	⎱ Head Escort to C in C 1st Corps not rly.	
" 28 "		
" 29 "	⎰	
" 30 "		
" 31 "		

26

Box 489

121/4196

B Squadron (2 Troops) S. Irish Horse.

Capt Trotter IVth C.B.

Vol I. December 1914 & January 1915

Decr. only.

IV.C

Cav

1914

Decg 1914

War Diary

Detachment South Irish Horse
(2 Troops) attached H.Q. 4th Corps

December 1914 and January 1915.

(1) Average Strength
- 3 Officers
- 77 Other Ranks
- Total 80

(2) Employment — Army Troops. Escorts. Orderlies. Police duties.

(3) Field operations — nil.

(4) Changes in Personnel

14 men joined from Base
1 man to Prison
1 man transferred to Squadron H.Q.
3 men to Hospital

Sheet No _____

PRINCESS MARY'S GIFTS.

Name of Unit, Detachment, or Hospital _____

NAMES IN ALPHABETICAL ORDER

Date _____

Commanding Officer.

(5). Changes in Horses.

    9 Horses joined from Base
    7 Horses cast as unfit
    1 Horse transferred to Sqn. HQ
    1 Horse died

(6). Report on Equipment, Clothing Saddlery - etc.

Satisfactory except.

    1. Riding Pants - dark Corduroy - are found much less serviceable than the Bedford Cord Pants first issued.

    2. Nose bags. canvas. wear out usually in a month.

4th Corps.
31. 1. 15

R. Blackett Capt
Comdg. Detachment
S. Irish Horse.

Sheet No _____

PRINCESS MARY'S GIFTS.

Name of Unit, Detachment, or Hospital _____

NAMES IN ALPHABETICAL ORDER

Date _____

Commanding Officer.

31/10/72

"15" Mr S ink chose
sent Lucy S 16
rd: 104

768/14

Army Form C. 2118

WAR DIARY
or
INTELLIGENCE SUMMARY
(Erase heading not required.)

B Squadron SOUTH IRISH HORSE
32nd Div. Cavalry.

Place	Date	Hour	Summary of Events and Information	Remarks and references to Appendices
HAVRE	25/11/15	6 am	Arrived from SOUTHAMPTON by SS "AFRICAN PRINCE" entrained at 6 pm.	
PONT REMY	26/11/15	5 am	detrained – marched to FAMECHON & billeted there	
FAMECHON	28/11/15	9 am	marched to OLINCOURT & billeted	
"	29/11/15		one horse died.	
FLESSELLES	1/12/15	10 am	marched to FLESSELLES & billeted. A party was employed daily for wood cutting and improving the billets with the R.E. The men were also practised in deepening rising.	
	7/12/15		one NCO proceeded to England, being commissioned	
BEHENCOURT	20/12/15	9 am	marched to BEHENCOURT (less Lieut G.C. COLVILL'S Troop which remained at FLESSELLES). The Squadron was employed daily in wood cutting in the Woods.	
"	22/12/15		one man joined the Troop at FLESSELLES from the base.	
"	27/12/15		" " " the Squadron at BEHENCOURT from the base.	
"	30/12/15		one horse died.	

Jeffcken Major
South Irish Horse

WAR DIARY
or
INTELLIGENCE SUMMARY

(Erase heading not required.)

Army Form C. 2118.

Hour, Date, Place	Summary of Events and Information	Remarks and references to Appendices.
Dec 1915. LE QUESNOY		
1	—	
2	⎱ men to Hospital ⎰ working on lines, cutting staff	
3	watching etc.	
4		
5		
6		
7		
8	1 man Hospital ⎱ not working in lines & clearing harness	
9		
10		
11		
12	1 man to ADC 1 & Colo Capt Watt (Engineers) with Capt Pugh took over Strategic. Capt Liddle, Lieut & Captain	
13	Squadron. Rain.	
14		
15		
16	men to Hospital & three extras mallein.	
17	Lunch on staffs relieving up.	
18	2 men to Hospital	
19		
20	Road reconnaissance for Division	
21		
22		
23		

WAR DIARY
or
INTELLIGENCE SUMMARY

Army Form C. 2118.

(Erase heading not required.)

Hour, Date, Place	Summary of Events and Information	Remarks and references to Appendices
Dec 1915 LE QUESNOY 24	} Inspection & Gunners training, foot drill.	
25		
26		
27		
28	10 Base reinforcements arrived from Base	
29	1 horse G.S.V.M.S. Cleaning refreshing for horses	
BEAUREPAIRE (LILLERS) 30	2/Lt Rueba taken on strength. Sqdn. moved (near Road T.E. moves) (S BEAUREPAIRE	
31	Cleaning near Billets—	

"B Seeead
S. Iresh
House
32nd
Vol. 3

Nov 15
May 16

MEMORANDUM.

Army Form C. 348.

From O.C. B Squadron
South Irish Horse (32nd Div Cavalry)

To D.A.G. G.H.Q.
       3rd Echelon

From

To

ANSWER.

In the field

March 24 1916.

_____ 191 .

Herewith War diaries for
months of December 1915 &
January 1916 of the above
Squadron as requested. These
diaries were sent before & I
cannot understand how they
went astray.

Jeff Stern Major
Commanding
B Squadron South Irish Horse

Army Form C. 2118

WAR DIARY
or
INTELLIGENCE SUMMARY
(Erase heading not required.)

A Squadron, South Irish Horse
32nd Divisional Cavalry

Place	Date	Hour	Summary of Events and Information	Remarks and references to Appendices
HAVRE	25/4/15	6 am	Arrived from SOUTHAMPTON by S.S. "AFRICAN PRINCE" entrained at 6 pm	
PONT REMY	26/4/15	5 am	Detrained & marched to FAMECHON & billeted there	
FAMECHON	28/4/15	9 am	Marched to OLINCOURT & billeted	
"	29/4/15	—	one horse died	
FLESSELLES	1/5/15	10 am	Marched to FLESSELLES & billeted, a party was employed daily for wood cutting & improving the billets with the R.E. The men were also practised in despatch riding	
"	7/5/15	—	one N.C.O. proceeded to England being commissioned	
BEHENCOURT	26/5/15	9 am	Marched to BEHENCOURT (2nd Lieut. J.C. Esthall's Troop which remained at FLESSELLES)	
"	"	—	The Squadron was employed daily in Woodcutting in the Woods	
"	22/6/15	—	one man joined the Troops at FLESSELLES from the Base	
"	27/6/15	—	" " " " Squadron at BEHENCOURT from the Base	
"	30/6/15	—	one horse died	

J C. J. Kerr Major.
Lt.Col. South Irish Horse

Army Form C. 2118

WAR DIARY
or
INTELLIGENCE SUMMARY
(Erase heading not required.)

"B" Squadron N.I. Horse
32nd Divisional Cavalry

Place	Date	Hour	Summary of Events and Information	Remarks and references to Appendices
BEHENCOURT	1/7/16	–	Squadron still billeted at BEHENCOURT. Fatigue cutting wood daily	
" "	2/7/16	–	Lieut COLVILL's troop rejoined Squadron from FIESSELLES	
" "	3/7/16	–	One horse transferred to 32nd Mobile Vet: Section. One man admitted to hospital owing to accident at wood cutting	
" "	6/7/16	–	One man suffering from Scarlet fever admitted to hospital, one horse transferred to 32nd Mobile Vet: Section	
" "	15/7/16	–	3 horses transferred to Mobile Vet: Section.	
" "	17/7/16	–	2nd Lieut BENCE-JONES Troop proceeded to SENLIS 32nd Div: Headquarters	
" "	24/7/16	–	One man admitted to hospital	
" "	29/7/16	–	One horse transferred to 32nd Div: Train. Woodcutting has been continued daily throughout the month.	

Jeffken Major
North Irish Horse

32nd Divisional Cavalry

"B" SQUADRON SOUTH IRISH HORSE

JANUARY 1 9 1 6

Army Form C. 2118

2nd Army

WAR DIARY

INTELLIGENCE SUMMARY

B Squadron SOUTH IRISH HORSE
32nd Div. Cavalry

(Erase heading not required.)

Instructions regarding War Diaries and Intelligence Summaries are contained in F.S. Regs., Part II. and the Staff Manual respectively. Title Pages will be prepared in manuscript.

Place	Date	Hour	Summary of Events and Information	Remarks and references to Appendices
BEHENCOURT	1.1.16		Squadron still billeted at BEHENCOURT. Fatigue cutting wood daily.	
"	2.1.16		Lieut COLVILL's troop rejoined Squadron from FLESSELLES.	
"	3.1.16		One horse transferred to 32nd Mobile Vet Section. One man admitted to Hosp. owing to accident at wood cutting.	
"	6.1.16		One man suffering from scarlet fever admitted to Hosp. One horse transferred to Mobile Vet Section.	
"	15.1.16		3 horses transferred to Mobile Vet Section.	
"	17.1.16		2nd Lieut BENCE JONES' troop proceeded to SENLIS, 32nd Div. Headquarters.	
"	24.1.16		One man admitted to Hosp.	
"	29.1.16		One horse transferred to 32nd Div. Train. Wood cutting has been continued daily throughout the month.	

Jeff Kern Major
Commanding B Squadron
SOUTH IRISH HORSE

32nd Divisional Cavalry

"B" SQUADRON SOUTH IRISH HORSE

FEBRUARY 1916

Army Form C. 2118

WAR DIARY
or
INTELLIGENCE SUMMARY
(Erase heading not required.)

B Squadron
SOUTH IRISH HORSE
32nd Division

Place	Date	Hour	Summary of Events and Information	Remarks and references to Appendices
BEHENCOURT	Feb 1		25 men employed cutting trees in the Wood daily.	
	" 3		6 Recruits joined. One horse transferred to Remount depot. 2nd Lieut N. JOYCE admitted to Field Ambulance. One horse transferred to Mobile Vet. Section. Lieut G. COLVILL's troop relieved 2nd Lieut C.W. BENCE-JONES' Troop at Div Headquarters at SENLIS	
"	" 13		One horse transferred to R.E. One horse died. A draft of 4 men joined from the Base. Lieut COLVILL's troop moved from SENLIS to HENENCOURT with Div H.Q.	
"	" 14		Three recruits joined	
"	" 18		2nd COVILL's troop relieved at Div. H.Q. by Sergt DALY's troop.	
	" 21		Three men joined Squadron from Base.	

Jeff Stern Major
South Irish Horse

Feb 29 1916

32nd Divisional Cavalry

"B" SQUADRON SOUTH IRISH HORSE

MARCH 1916

Army Form C. 2118

WAR DIARY
INTELLIGENCE SUMMARY
(Erase heading not required.)

B Squadron SOUTH IRISH HORSE
32nd Divisional Cavalry

Place	Date	Hour	Summary of Events and Information	Remarks and references to Appendices
BEHENCOURT	1.3.16		The Squadron continued to be employed in the woods cutting trees.	
"	2.3.16		2nd Lieut DIGNAN'S Troop relieved Sergt DALY'S Troop at Div. Headquarters at HENENCOURT	
"	3.3.16		The Sergt and 17 men proceeded to TALMAS for threshing.	
"	7.3.16		One Sergt and 8 men proceeded to HENENCOURT to be attached to M.M.P. 32nd Division	
"	10.3.16		Two NCOs proceeded to WISQUES for course in the HOTCHKISS gun. One horse died.	
"	15.3.16		The two NCOs returned from course of instruction at WISQUES.	
"	18.3.16		Two remounts joined.	
"	19.3.16		Lieut BENCE-JONE'S Troop relieved 2nd Lieut DIGNAN'S Troop at HENENCOURT.	
"	21.3.16		One Sergt 17 men returned to Squadron Headquarters from TALMAS.	
"	26.3.16		One man proceeded to England (commissioned). One man proceeded to Refilling Casualty Clearing Station	
"	31.3.16		One horse transferred to 42nd Mobile Vet. Section.	

J.F. St Keene Major
South Irish Horse

32nd Divisional Cavalry

"B" SQUADRON SOUTH IRISH HORSE

APRIL 1916

Vol. 5

Army Form C.2118

WAR DIARY or INTELLIGENCE SUMMARY

(Erase heading not required.)

B Squadron SOUTH IRISH HORSE
32nd Div. Cavalry 32

Place	Date	Hour	Summary of Events and Information	Remarks and references to Appendices
BEHENCOURT	1/4/16		The Squadron still engaged in the same place and working parties continued their work in the woods. One NCO was admitted to hospital with a strained leg from kick from horse.	
"	3/4/16		2nd Troop relieved 4th Troop at Div. Headquarters which removed from HENENCOURT to SENLIS this day. 2nd Lieut W JOYCE separated from Squadron.	
"	4/4/16		2nd Lieut JOYCE rejoined his Troop at SENLIS. One horse transferred to 32nd Mobile Vet Section.	
"	7/4/16		The Squadron moved to CONTAY and took on billets vacated by 36th Div Cavalry. One horse transferred to Mobile Vet Section.	
"	13/4/16		Four NCOs went to the trenches for 4 days tour of duty. 2 men + 3 horses were attached to no. 4 Squadron Royal Flying Corps at BELLE AIR FARM & estationed in the 27/4/16. Sergt DALY proceeded on to the Base leave expired. One horse joined from 15th Bn LANCASHIRE FUSILIERS.	
"	14/4/16			
"	17/4/16		S.S.M. LARKIN + one NCO proceeded to CAMIERS for Machine gun course returning on 25/4/16	
"	18/4/16		2nd Lieut DIGNAN'S Troop relieved 2nd Lieut JOYCE'S Troop at SENLIS.	
	19/4/16			
	20/4/16		1 Horse transferred to Mobile Vet Section.	
	25/4/16		One man proceeded to base time expired.	
	29/4/16		One horse transferred to Mobile Vet Section.	
	30/4/16		3 remounts joined the Squadron.	

Jeff Keim Major
South Irish Horse

32nd Divisional Cavalry

BECAME XVth CORPS CAVALRY 14.5.16.

"B" SQUADRON SOUTH IRISH HORSE

M A Y 1 9 1 6

Army Form C. 2118

WAR DIARY
or
INTELLIGENCE SUMMARY
(Erase heading not required.)

B Squadron SOUTH IRISH HORSE
XV Corps Cavalry Regiment

Vol. 6

Place	Date	Hour	Summary of Events and Information	Remarks and references to Appendices
CONTAY	1/5/16		The Squadron was still employed in Forestry work for the 32nd Division; one troop being with Divisional Headquarters.	
"	2/5/16		One man evacuated to South Midland Casualty Clearing Station.	
"	3/5/16		Lieut COLVILL'S Troop relieved 2nd Lieut DIGNAN'S Troop at Div. H.Q at SENLIS.	
"	4/5/16		One man evacuated to S.M. Casualty Clearing Station.	
"	5/5/16		Sergt-Farrier BUTLER proceeded to U.K. his time expired.	
"	9/5/16		2 horses evacuated to 42nd MOBILE VET. Section.	
"	10/5/16		One man evacuated to S.M. Casualty Clearing Station.	
"	14/5/16		The Squadron moved to HEILLY on transfer to XV Corps as Corps Cavalry Regt- composed of A, B Squadrons SOUTH IRISH HORSE & C Squadron SURREY YEOMANRY. 32 NCO's & men proceeded to RIBEMONT to be attached to 21st DIVISION as M.M. POLICE. A party proceeded daily to BRAY for work in connection with gun epuirements.	
HEILLY	17/5/16		One man joined from Base.	
"	22/5/16		Lieut BENCE-JONES & 2 batmen proceeded to the Cavalry School 2nd Indian Cavalry Division for a course of instruction at GAMACHE	
"	23/5/16		2 men transferred to the Corps of M.M. POLICE 32nd Division	
"	27/5/16		One horse " " " " " 12" Mobile Vet Section	
"	28/5/16		" " " " " "	
"	31/5/16		One troop under Lieut JOYCE commenced Troop training	

J.J. Stearne Major
South Irish Horse

www.ingramcontent.com/pod-product-compliance
Lightning Source LLC
Chambersburg PA
CBHW081501160426
43193CB00013B/2557

First World War
and Army of Occupation
War Diary
France, Belgium and Germany

74 (YEOMANRY) DIVISION
229 Infantry Brigade
Prince Albert's (Somerset Light Infantry)
12th Battalion
1 May 1918 - 20 June 1919

WO95/3152/3

The Naval & Military Press Ltd
www.nmarchive.com
Published in association with The National Archives

Published by

The Naval & Military Press Ltd

Unit 10 Ridgewood Industrial Park,

Uckfield, East Sussex,

TN22 5QE England

Tel: +44 (0) 1825 749494

www.naval-military-press.com

www.nmarchive.com

This diary has been reprinted in facsimile from the original. Any imperfections are inevitably reproduced and the quality may fall short of modern type and cartographic standards.

© **Crown Copyright**
Images reproduced by permission of The National Archives, London, England, 2015.

Contents

Document type	Place/Title	Date From	Date To
Heading	WO95/3152/3 12 Battalion Somerset Light Infantry		
Heading	74th Division 229th Infy Bde 12th Bn Som Light Infy 1918 May-Jun 1919		
Miscellaneous	HQ 229 Bde Herewith War Diary For Month of May	02/06/1918	02/06/1918
War Diary	H.M.S.T Leasowe Castle	01/05/1918	10/05/1918
War Diary	Forest Montiers	11/05/1918	20/05/1918
War Diary	Sus St Leger	21/05/1918	25/05/1918
War Diary	Lignereuil	26/05/1918	29/05/1918
War Diary	Lignereuil Map Ref France Sheet 51c I 21 1/40,000	30/05/1918	31/05/1918
War Diary	Lignereuil	01/06/1918	26/06/1918
War Diary	Rely	26/06/1918	26/06/1918
War Diary	Ref Map Sheet 36a 1/40,000	26/06/1918	11/07/1918
War Diary	Ref Map Sheet 36 A 1/40000 O.30.c O.36.a O.35.c	12/07/1918	22/07/1918
War Diary	Ref Map France Sheet 36a 1/40000 La Miquelleris (O.36a)	23/07/1918	23/07/1918
War Diary	Ref Map Sheet 36a 1/40000 France	24/07/1918	31/07/1918
Miscellaneous	H.Q.229 Bde Herewith War Diary For Month of August	06/09/1918	06/09/1918
War Diary	Ref Map France Sheet 36a 1/40000	01/08/1918	04/08/1918
War Diary	Ref Map France Sheet 36a S.E 1/20000	05/08/1918	14/08/1918
War Diary	Ref Map Sheet 36a France 1/40000	15/08/1918	16/08/1918
War Diary	Guarbecque	17/08/1918	18/08/1918
War Diary	Ref Map France Sheet 36a 1/40000	19/08/1918	19/08/1918
War Diary	Guarbecque	20/08/1918	22/08/1918
War Diary	Ref Map France Sheet 36a 1/40000	23/08/1918	25/08/1918
War Diary	Ref Map France Sheet 36a	26/08/1918	27/08/1918
War Diary	Manqueville	28/08/1918	28/08/1918
War Diary	Map Ref France Sheet 36a 1/40000	29/08/1918	29/08/1918
War Diary	Amiens 17 1/100000	30/08/1918	31/08/1918
War Diary	Map Ref France Sheet 62c NW 1/20000	01/09/1918	06/09/1918
War Diary	Ref Map Sheet 62c N.E. 1/20000	07/09/1918	25/09/1918
War Diary	Ref Map Sheet 62c 1/40000	26/09/1918	30/09/1918
Heading	HQ. 229th Infty Bde		
War Diary	Ref Map France Sheet 36a 1/40000	01/10/1918	03/10/1918
War Diary	Sheet 36 S.W. 1/20000	03/10/1918	05/10/1918
War Diary	Map Ref France Sheet 36 S.W.1/20000	06/10/1918	17/10/1918
War Diary	Map Ref France Sheet 36 S.W.1/20000 & Sheet 36SE	17/10/1918	17/10/1918
War Diary	Map Ref Sheet 37 S.E. 1/40000	18/10/1918	20/10/1918
War Diary	Ref Map Sheet 37 S.W. 1/20000	21/10/1918	28/10/1918
Miscellaneous	H.Q. 229th Infy Bde	01/01/1918	01/01/1918
War Diary	Ref Map Sheet 37 S.W. 1/20000	29/10/1918	31/10/1918
Heading	HQ 229th Infy Bde		
War Diary	Ref Map France Sheet 37	01/11/1918	10/11/1918
War Diary	Ref Map France Sheet 37 1/40000	11/11/1918	11/11/1918
War Diary	Belgium Sheet 38 1/40000	12/11/1918	12/11/1918
War Diary	Ref Map Belgium Sheet 38	14/11/1918	17/11/1918
War Diary	Ref Map Sheet 38 Belgium 1/40000 Sheet 37	18/11/1918	24/11/1918
War Diary	Ref Map Belgium Sheet 37 1/40000 Sheet 37	25/11/1918	30/11/1918
Miscellaneous	D.A.G. 3rd Echelon	10/01/1919	10/01/1919
War Diary	Map Ref Belgium Sheet 37 1/40000	01/12/1918	19/12/1918

War Diary	Map Ref Sheet 30 1/40000	20/12/1918	14/01/1919
War Diary	Ref Map Belgium Sheet 30 1/40000	15/01/1919	28/02/1919
Heading	HQ 229th Infy Bde		
War Diary	Ref Map Belgium Sheet 30 1/40000	01/03/1919	31/03/1919
Heading	H.Q. 229th Infty Bde		
War Diary	Ref Map Belgium Sheet 30 1/40000	01/04/1919	14/06/1919
War Diary	Sheet 30 1/40000	16/06/1919	20/06/1919

WO95/3152/3

12 Battalion Somerset Light Infantry

74TH DIVISION
229TH INFY BDE

12TH BN SOM. LIGHT INFY.
1918 MAY - ~~DEC 1918~~
~~JAN~~ - JUN 1919

HQ 229 Bde

Herewith WAR DIARY for month of MAY please

2/6/18

R.T. Domnett
Capt.
Adj. 12 (West-Som Yeo) Battn S.L.I.

May 1/18

Army Form C. 2118.

WAR DIARY
or
INTELLIGENCE SUMMARY

(Erase heading not required). 13/ West Somerset 4(R) Battn SLI

Vol 2

Place	Date	Hour	Summary of Events and Information	Remarks and references to Appendices.
H.M.S.T. "LEASOWE CASTLE".	May 1918			
	1	1030	Inspection of troop decks.	
		1000	General parade. Practice gas drill	
		1500	Battn came on ship's duty. 5 Officers, 232 O.R. on duty.	
	2	1030	Inspection of troop decks.	
		1400	General parade. Practice gas drill. Practice alarm, all ranks at alarm post under 4 minutes	
	3	1030	Inspection of troop decks.	
		1100	General parade Practice gas drill. Medical inspection.	
	4	1030	Inspection of troop decks.	
		1100	General parade and gas drill. Practice fire alarm.	
		1600	Battn came on duty. Clocks put back 20 minutes at 1000 - 1400 and 1900.	

E.L. Polk Lt Col
Commanding 13 (W.S.) Bn SLI

Army Form C. 2118.

WAR DIARY
or
INTELLIGENCE SUMMARY.

(Erase heading not required). 12 (West Somerset Yeo) Battn S.L.I

Place	Date	Hour	Summary of Events and Information	Remarks and references to Appendices.
H.M.S.T. "LEASOWE CASTLE".	May 1918 5.		Inspection of troop decks.	
	6.	1030	General parade and Gas drill. Voluntary service 1030.	
			Inspection of troop decks. General parade and gas drill.	
"	7.		Arrived MARSEILLES at 0700. Disembarked at 2100 and marched to station, entraining at 2300.	
"	8.		Train left station at 0300 enroute for NOYELLES.	
"	9.		In train en route for NOYELLES.	
"	10.		Arrived at NOYELLES at 1430. Detrained at 1500 and marched to billets at FOREST MONTIERS.	
FOREST MONTIERS	11.		Billets at FOREST MONTIERS. Parades under Company Commanders. "C" Coy had use of baths.	

G.C. Pope Lt Col
Commanding 12 (W.S.Y) Bn S.L.I

Army Form C. 2118.

WAR DIARY
INTELLIGENCE SUMMARY

12 (West Somerset Yeomanry) Batt. S.L.I.

Place	Date	Hour	Summary of Events and Information	Remarks and references to Appendices.
FOREST MONTIERS	12.	0800	"C"&"D" Coys Gas drill under Corps Gas instructors.	
		1330	All ranks lectured by Corps Gas Officer. "B" Coy had use of baths. A Coy parades under Coy arrangements	
		1400	D Coy had use of baths. A & B Coys Gas drill under Corps Gas Instructors.	
	13.		Voluntary Service at 0730 and 1730.	
"		0800	"A" Coy. H.Q. and details had use of baths.	
		1400	Parades under Coy Commanders.	
"	14.	0800	H.Q. A & B Coys. Route march. C & D. Coys under Coy arrangements. Specialists classes continued.	
"	15.		H.Q A & B Coy under Coy Commanders. C & D route march. Specialist classes continued. The Bath this day was completed with Chargers and transport viz Chargers. 11. Transport Pack animals 44. Vehicles wagons L.G.S. 10. Field Kitchens 4. Water Carts 2. Cooks carts 1. Malter Cart 1. Bicycles 4.	

G. M. Sale Lt Col
Commanding 12 (W.Sy) Bn S.L.I.

Army Form C. 2118.

WAR DIARY
or
INTELLIGENCE SUMMARY.

(Erase heading not required). 12 (West Somerset Yeomanry) Battalion Som L I

Place	Date	Hour	Summary of Events and Information	Remarks and references to Appendices.
FOREST FRONTIERS/6	May 1918		Parades at 0500 & 1400 under Company Commanders. Specialists classes continued. 1000 Col Campbell lectured to the Battn on Physical Training and Bayonet fighting.	
		1400	Lt Col Tempsley D.S.O. G.S.O.1 74th (Yeo) Div lectured to Commanding Officers, Adjutants, and Company Commanders of the Bde.	
	17		Parades at 8 AM and 2 PM under Company Commanders. Specialist Classes continued. A class in train reserve sketches tracing was commenced this day.	
			Strength decrease 1 O.R. to Hospital	
	18	9 AM	Parades under Company Commanders.	
		8.30	C.O. inspected all transport & personnel on leaving Emma	
		9.10	"B" Coy at disposal of Baffo Gas Officer	
		9.15	The C.O. inspected "A" Coy on the parade field.	

G. P. Nosle Lt Col
Commanding 12 (W.S.Y) Bn S L I

Army Form C. 2118.

WAR DIARY
or
INTELLIGENCE SUMMARY.

12th (West Somerset Yeo) Batt'n Som L I

Place	Date	Hour	Summary of Events and Information	Remarks and references to Appendices.
FOREST MONTIERS	MAY 1918 (Cont) 18	10.30 AM	Battalion three under the Commands Officer on Parning Ground	
		2.P.M.	Lecture to all Officers by Capt A.H. Wheeler M.C. on The Tactical use of the Lewis Gun.	
		9.P.M.	Gas Projector demonstration at ROMIOTTE by Major Brait.	
	19	8 A.M	Parades under Coy Commanders. Specialists classes continued.	
			"D" Coy at disposal of Batt'n gas officer from 9 to 10 A.M. "A" Coy from 10 to 11 Billeting party sent forward to Sus St LEGER.	
	20		Parades under Coy Commanders. 26 officers 647 OR marched from FOREST MONTIERS at 7 P.M. to RUE and entrained at 9 P.M. with whole of transport.	
SUS ST LEGER	21		Arrived at LIGNY ST FLOCHEL at 2.40 A.M. detrained and marched to SUS ST LEGER. 9.30 A.M. remainder of Batt'n entrained to RUE ft. LIGNY ST FLOCHEL and marched to Sus St LEGER.	
	22		Parades at 9 AM and 2 P.M. under Coy Commanders.	
	23	9 A.M	A & B Coys and C & D carried out a tactical exercises Specialists classes continued.	

E M Boe / Lt Col
Commanding 12 (W.S.Y) Bn S L I

Army Form C. 2118.

WAR DIARY
or
INTELLIGENCE SUMMARY

(Erase heading not required). 1/2 (West Somerset Yeo) Battn. Som Light Infty.

Place	Date	Hour	Summary of Events and Information	Remarks and references to Appendices.
SUS ST LEGER.	24		"A" Coy & HQ Route march under Capt E.F.S. Rodd. B, C & D Coys under Coy Commanders. Sergt. Maj. Tyrrell. Army Gymnastic Staff saw B, C & D Coys for an hour each Coy at Bayonet fighting and Physical Training. Instructional classes continued. 2/Lt Hallowell admitted to Hosp.	
	25		The Battalion marched from SUS ST LEGER at 0545 to LIGNEREUIL. Arrived at 10.30 and went into billets. 2/Lt Cross appointed Battn Scout officer.	
LIGNEREUIL	26.		Parades under Coy Commanders. Instructional classes continued. Holy Communion at 7.11 AM. Evening Service (voluntary) 7 PM.	
	27.		The Battn was inspected at 9.15 AM by the G.O.C. 74th Division.	
	28.		Battalion parades under Coy Commanders. Parades under Coy Commanders, special attention being given to Wood fighting. "B" Coy had march. Instructional classes continued.	
	29.		"A" Coy Bathing at HQ BERLENCOURT. "C" Coy in charge of MANIN. B Coy under Coy Commdt. D Coy Bathing at BERLENCOURT. Instructional classes continued.	

E.N. Rose Lt Col.
Commanding 12 (West Som Yeo) Battn SLI.

Army Form C. 2118.

WAR DIARY
or
INTELLIGENCE SUMMARY.

(Erase heading not required). 12 (West Somerset Yeo) Battn Som Light Infy

Instructions regarding War Diaries and Intelligence Summaries are contained in F.S. Regs., Part II. and the Staff Manual respectively. Title pages will be prepared in manuscript.

Place	Date	Hour	Summary of Events and Information	Remarks and references to Appendices.
LIGNEREUIL Map Ref France Sheet 51 c I.21 4/40000	30.	9 A.M 8″ 8″ 8″	Instructional classes continued. A & D Coys Tactical exercise. B. Coy on range. C Coy under Coy Commander.	
	31.	8″	Instructional classes continued. B. C Coys and details bathing at BERLECOURT. A & D Coys under Coy Com	
		1-30 P.M.	Battn Tactical exercise under the Commanding Officer.	

Daily Strength.

	Off.	OR.			
1	35.	961.	13	34.	948.
2	35.	961.	14	34.	946.
3	35.	961.	15	34.	945.
4	35.	961.	16	34.	944.
5	35.	962.	17	34.	939.
6	35.	962.	18	34.	936.
7	35.	962.	19	34.	931.
8	35.	962.	20	35.	930.
9	35.	962.	21	35.	928.
10	35.	962.	22	35.	928.
11	35.	956.	23	36.	931.
12	35.	954.	24	36.	916.

25.	35.	908.
26.	34.	905.
27.	34.	903.
28.	34.	901.
29.	34.	894.
30.	34.	886.
31.	33.	869.

C. J. [signature]
Lt Col.
Commanding 12 (W.S.Y) Bn S.L.I.

WAR DIARY
or
INTELLIGENCE SUMMARY.

(Erase heading not required). 12th (West Somerset Yeomanry) Battn Som L.I.

Army Form C. 2118.
June 1918

Place	Date	Hour	Summary of Events and Information	Remarks and references to Appendices.
LIGNEREUIL	June 1918			
	1.		Infr Brigade Tactical Exercise. 231st Brigade defending 229 Bde attacking. The Battn was in the front line and attacked on a two Coy frontage on the left of the Bde, drove the enemy from his position, occupied and held the enemy line pushing out patrols and Lewis Guns.	
	2.		Communion at 7 AM Evening Service 7 PM.	
	3.		Parades at 8 AM and 1.30 PM under Coy Commanders. Instructional classes continued. "A" Coy threw live bombs.	
	4.		Battalion Tactical exercise. G.O.C. 1st Tank Bde lectured to Officers of the Battn on "Co-operation between Infantry and Tanks". Instructional classes continued.	
	5.		Battn route march. Demonstration by Tanks. All ranks armed with a rifle did range practice.	

R.S. Poole, Lt Col
Commanding 12 (W.S.Y.) Bn S.L.I.

Army Form C. 2118.

WAR DIARY
or
INTELLIGENCE SUMMARY.

(Erase heading not required.) 12th (West Somerset Yeomanry) Battn S L I

Place	Date	Hour	Summary of Events and Information	Remarks and references to Appendices.
LIGNEREUIL	JUNE 1918			
	6.		Parades under Company Commanders. "A" Coy on "C" range at MANIN. Instructional classes continued. "B" Coy (two platoons) threw live bombs.	
	7.		Brigade Tactical Exercise. The Battn at the first stage were in Bde Reserve. After first objective passed the Battn Bn frogged through and advanced on second objective. 2nd Lt. JENKINS joined the Bn for duty. Instructional	
	8.		Parades under Coy Commanders. Instructional classes continued. A.B & C Coys had use of baths at GRAND RULLECOURT. 2 2Lts. HEWETT & POWIS joined the Bn for duty.	
	9.		Voluntary service at 7 A.M. 8.30 A.M. and 7.30.P.M. The Commanding Officer inspected the Battalion Transport at 2.30. P.M.	

G Poole
Lt Col.
Commanding 12(WSY)Bn S L I

Army Form C. 2118.

WAR DIARY
or
INTELLIGENCE SUMMARY.

(Erase heading not required). 12 (West Somerset Yeo) Battn. Somerset Light Infantry.

Place	Date	Hour	Summary of Events and Information	Remarks and references to Appendices.
LIGNEREUIL	June 1918.			
	10	8 A.M.	Parades under Coy Commanders. Instructional classes continued. "D" on range at MANIN. "C" Coy and two platoons "B" Coy threw live bombs.	
		1-30 P.M.	A Coy and two platoons each of B & C Coy practised an advance with Tanks. Riding school for junior officers. "C" Coy on range.	
	11.		Parades contd. Coy Commanders. Tactical exercise under Capt A.H.WHEELER. corporating Wood and village fighting. Instructional classes continued. Riding school for junior offrs.	
	12		Parades under Company Commanders. 6 P.M. 2Lt Brown lectured Instructional classes continued. Riding school for all officers on encoding and decoding. Riding school for junior officers.	
	13.		Instructional classes continued. The Bn witnessed a practice attack with Tanks and Infantry.	

R.S. Poole
Lt Col
Commanding 12 (W.S.Y.) Bn. S.L.I.

A.P. & S.D., Alex./ 2000/11:17/5M. W.M. & Co.
50025A

Army Form C. 2118.

WAR DIARY
or
INTELLIGENCE SUMMARY.

(Erase heading not required.) 1/2(West Somerset Yeomanry) Bn Somerset L.I

Instructions regarding War Diaries and Intelligence Summaries are contained in F. S. Regs., Part II. and the Staff Manual respectively. Title pages will be prepared in manuscript.

Place	Date	Hour	Summary of Events and Information	Remarks and references to Appendices
LIGNEREUIL	14 June 1918		Parades under Company Commanders. C&D Coy had use of baths and disinfector. A GRAND RULLECOURT. "A" Coy field bin bombs with the new grenade discharger. Instructional classes continued.	
	15		C&D Coy Bn scouts and signallers took part in an Bde Brigade Tactical exercise. 236th Bde attacked the 239 hit Bde defended bringing out the counter-attack. A&B Coy had use of baths and disinfector at Grand Rullecourt.	
	16	7.45 A.M.	Holy Communion at 7.45 A.M. Voluntary Service at 6 P.M.	
	17		All scouts, snipers and observers had use of "A" range. Parades under Coy Commanders. Instructional classes contd. "B" Coy had use of 30 yds grenade discharger range at 8. A.M. "C" " " " " " " " " - 2 P.M. 2/Lt. TABOR. RICHARDS, joined the Bn for duty. Lt. BROWN M.C. joined the Bn for duty.	
	18		Bn Tactical Exercise. A&B Coy V. C&D Coy, the former two Coys attacked, the latter defended and counter-attacked.	

R.C. Poole
Lt Col.
Commanding 1/2(W.S.Y)Bn.S.L.I.

WAR DIARY
INTELLIGENCE SUMMARY

(Erase heading not required.) 1/2 (West Som't Yeo) Bn Somerset Light Infty

Army Form C. 2118.

Instructions regarding War Diaries and Intelligence Summaries are contained in F. S. Regs., Part II. and the Staff Manual respectively. Title pages will be prepared in manuscript.

Place	Date	Hour	Summary of Events and Information	Remarks and references to Appendices
			June 1918	
LIGNEREUIL	19.		Parades under Company Commanders. Instructional classes continued. "C" Coy had use of Bayonet fighting course in the morning. D. in the afternoon. Riding School for Junior Officers. Lectures by Commanding Officer to all officers, NCOs and Section Leaders. A & B Coy practiced night operations.	
	20.		Parades under Coy Commanders. Instructional classes continued. "C" Range allotted to "C" Coy. "A" Coy in the morning and D Coy the afternoon had use of the Bayonet fighting course. Riding school for Junior officers.	
	21.		The Bn less "B" Coy went for a route march route:- BLAVINCOURT - APPEGRENEE - BEAUFORT - GIVENCHY LE - NOBLE. "B" Coy on "A" range. Bde Tactical Exercise. The Bn took up a line of defence in the BOIS-A- ROSERMONT. The remainder of Bde attached. A & D Coys were in the front line. "C" Coy in support. B. Coy in reserve.	
	22.			
	23.		Holy Communion at 8. A.M. Voluntary Evening Service at 7.P.M. Parades under Coy Commanders. Instructional classes continued.	
	24.		B. Coy had use of Bayonet fighting course in the morning C Coy in the afternoon. A & D Coys to Galeb near SBR in Coo.	

E.W. Noble Lt Col
Commanding 12 (W.S.Y) Bn Som L.I.

Army Form C. 2118.

WAR DIARY
or
INTELLIGENCE SUMMARY

(Erase heading not required.) 1/2nd (West) Somerset Yeomany/2nd Somerset Light Infantry

Instructions regarding War Diaries and Intelligence Summaries are contained in F. S. Regs., Part II. and the Staff Manual respectively. Title pages will be prepared in manuscript.

Place	Date	Hour	Summary of Events and Information	Remarks and references to Appendices
	June 1918.			
LIGNEREUIL	25.		Parades under Coy Commanders. Instructional classes continued. "C" Coy. H.Q. and Transport tested S.B.R. in gas. At 2.P.M. The Bn was given practice with contact aeroplane, in finding the height, aiming at it and putting up an imaginary barrage etc.	
LIGNEREUIL	26.		The Bde moved to the WITTERNESSE - MAZINGHEM area. The Bn paraded at 7.45AM	
RELY Ref Map Sheet 36a 1/40000		11.15	arriving at AIRE about 3.30 PM. detrained and marched to RELY arriving about 8 PM. and went into billets. The transport came by road.	
	27.		Parades under Coy Commanders. Cleaning billets and billeting areas. Recreational games.	
	28.		Parades under Coy Commanders. Instructional classes continued	
"	29.		Bn HQ, A & D Coys marched to bivouac in J25a. Coming under orders of S.I. Corps 9.5 am. "B" Coy marched to BUSNES (P.32.) coming under orders of 61st Divn for work. "C" Coy marched to STEVENANT (P.10.) coming under orders of 61st Divn for work.	

E.G. Poole Lt Col
Commanding 12 (W.S.) Bn SL.I.

Army Form C. 2118.

WAR DIARY
or
INTELLIGENCE SUMMARY.
(Erase heading not required.) 1/2 T.H. (West Somerset Yeomanry) Battn Som L.I.

Instructions regarding War Diaries and Intelligence Summaries are contained in F. S. Regs., Part II. and the Staff Manual respectively. Title pages will be prepared in manuscript.

Place	Date	Hour	Summary of Events and Information	Remarks and references to Appendices
Rfr Mob Shed Sta. 30	June 1918.			
			Pri Hen Drs, A+D Coys bivouaced in T25 a.	
			"B" Coy at BUSNES. "C" Coy at ST VENANT.	
			Work under R.Es.	
			OR OR	
	1.		33 868	
	2.		32 853	
	3.		34 833	
	4.		32 845	
	5.		36 849	
	6.		35 830	
	7.		29 834	
	8.		30 836	
	9.		31 803	
	10.		30 797	
	11.		33 775	
	12.		32 745	
	13.		33 757	
	14.		32 750	
	15.		32 751	
	16.		33 841	
	17.		34 844	
	18.		32 758	
	19.		32 763	
	20.		31 766	
	21.		31 778	
	22.		30 791	
	23.		29 808	
	24.		29 785	
	25.		28 801	
	26.		27 794	
	27.		29 807	
	28.		27 790	
	29.		24 770	
	30.		23 751	

E.C. Rose
Lt Col.
Commdg 12th (W.S.Y.) Bn Som L.I.

Army Form C. 2118.

WAR DIARY
or
INTELLIGENCE SUMMARY.
(Erase heading not required.)

12th (WSY) Bn Somerset L.I. July /18

Place	Date	Hour	Summary of Events and Information	Remarks and references to Appendices
Map Ref Sheet 36a 1/40000	July 1.		A & D Coys & Bn Head Qrs in bivouac at T25 a	
			B Coy billeted in BUSNES (P26 c0.3)	
			C Coy " " ST VENANT (P9 d 4.10)	
	2	7am 6pm	A Coy work under R.E. 5th Bn Ty. D " " " R.E. XI Corps. B & C Coys work under R.E. 61st Divn Strength increase 3 O.R. from 1st Bn Somt L.I. 2 O.R. from 7th Bn Somt L.I.	
			Bn relieved as on 1st inst. work under R.Es as above.	
	3	8am	Strength increase 5 O.R. from 7th Som L.I. 3 O.R. from 8th Som L.I. 2 O.R. from 6th Som L.I. 1 O.R. from 1st Som L.I. A reconnaissance was carried out of the Reserve line by 30 Officers & O.Rs	
			Bn relieved as above. Work under R.Es by all available men of Companies. Reconnaissance of the LILLIERS - STEENBECQUE LINE was made by 30 Officers & O.Rs.	

C.D. Heyworth Lt Col
for Lt Col
Commdg 12th (WSY) Bn.

Army Form C. 2118.

WAR DIARY
or
INTELLIGENCE SUMMARY.
(Erase heading not required.) 12th (W.S.) Bttn Somerset L.I.

Instructions regarding War Diaries and Intelligence Summaries are contained in F. S. Regs., Part II. and the Staff Manual respectively. Title pages will be prepared in manuscript.

Place	Date	Hour	Summary of Events and Information	Remarks and references to Appendices
Hd Qrs Sect 36 Yones	July 4.		Disposition of Bn as on 3rd. Work under R.E. as on previous day. A reconnaissance of the newly captured line was repeated. Strength increase 1. OR from 1st Som L.I. 2 OR from 9th Som L.I. 1 OR from 7th Som L.I.	
	5.		Disposition of Bn as before. Work under REs as before. A reconnaissance of the BUSNES-SEENABECQUE line was repeated by 30 officers & ORs. During night of 4/5. shelling of Bn transport lines took place. ORs killed 4. ORs wounded 5. Horses killed. Officers charger 1. N.D.2. Capt R.C. Doyle received to be attached to Ul (London Gazette 12.6.16) Strength increase. 3 OR from 6th Bttn Som L.I. 7 ORs from 7th Som L.I. 3 OR from 8th Som L.I.	
	6.		Disposition of Bn as before. Work under REs as usual. A reconnaissance of BUSNES-SEENABECQUE LINE was repeated. 2nd Lts GRIMSHAW & WILDE & Q.O.R. proceed to XI Corps School for Courses.	

E.M. Morgan Major
Commanding 12th (W.S.) Bn Som L.I.

Army Form C. 2118.

WAR DIARY
or
INTELLIGENCE SUMMARY.
(Erase heading not required.)

125/(WSY)/R2 Somerset L.I.

Instructions regarding War Diaries and Intelligence Summaries are contained in F. S. Regs., Part II. and the Staff Manual respectively. Title pages will be prepared in manuscript.

Place	Date	Hour	Summary of Events and Information	Remarks and references to Appendices
Ref Map & Sheet 36a Yucorp.	July 7.	9am 2pm 5.15 pm	Disposition of Bn as before. Work under R.E.s was continued. Reconnaissance of Anusoires - Haverskerque - La Motte Line carried out by 30 officers & O.R. Voluntary bathing parade under an officer. Voluntary divine service (Cof E) near camp of A & D Coys & HQrs.	
	8.		Disposition of Bn as before. Work under R.E.s was continued. Reconnaissance of Anusoires - Haverskerque - La Motte Line repeated by 30 officers & OR.	
	9.		Disposition of Bn as y'day. Work under R.E.s continued. Reconnaissance of the Lilliers - Steenbecque Line by 30 officers & N.C.O.	
	10.		Disposition of Bn as before. Work under R.E.s was discontinued. Parade under Coy. Commanders. "B" Coy. proceeded to Witternesse. Strength decrease, 2nd Lt Griffiths invalided to England & 4 OR.	
	11.	9am	The HQr moved to La Miquellerie & La Flandrie (O30c, O36a & b, O31c) H.Qrs., B, C & D Coys at La Miquellerie & "A" Coy at La Flandrie.	

C.O. Wyndham Lt Col
Cmdg 125th (WSy) Bn Som L.I.

Army Form C. 2118.

WAR DIARY
or
INTELLIGENCE SUMMARY.
(Erase heading not required.) 12th (WSy) Rl Sussex L.I.

Instructions regarding War Diaries and Intelligence Summaries are contained in F. S. Regs., Part II. and the Staff Manual respectively. Title pages will be prepared in manuscript.

Place	Date	Hour	Summary of Events and Information	Remarks and references to Appendices
REF MAP SHEET 36A. Y40.d.0. C30.c. 030.a.l. C33.c.	July 12.	5.15 8 am 1.30 pm	Physical drawing. Parades under Coy Commanders	
"	13.		The BN had the use of the Baths at HAM EN ARTOIS. Parades under Coy Commanders. Strength decrease. 1 Pvt BROWN M.C. to XI Corps School, as Instructor.	
"	14.		Coys at disposal of Coy Commanders. Divine Service Coy E. 9 am & 7 pm.	
"	15.		The Commanding Officer inspected B, C & D Companies. Instructional classes were continued.	
"	16.	10 am	The C.R.E. XI Corps congratulates the 74 Aust on excellent work carried out by the Bn during the last fortnight. Strength increase 27 O.Rs from 52nd Grad Hants. The Commanding Officer inspected "A" Company. Other parades under Coy Commanders. Instructional classes continued.	

C.O. Majoring
officer
for Lt Col.
Command 12th (WSy) Rn S.L.I.

Army Form C. 2118.

WAR DIARY
or
INTELLIGENCE SUMMARY.

(Erase heading not required.) 12B (W.S.) B.N. Somerset L.I.

Place	Date	Hour	Summary of Events and Information	Remarks and references to Appendices
Rue Hue Sheet 36ª 1/40000 O 30 c O 36 a + b O 35 c	JULY 17.		Parades under Coy arrangements. Instructional classes continued. Reconnaissance of AMUSOIRES - HAVERSKERQUE LINE by Officers & N.C.Os.	
	18		Batt had use of Baths at HAM EN ARTOIS. Parades under Coy Commanders. Instructional classes continued.	
"	19.		Parades under Coy arrangements. Practice skeleton Bde scheme "New battle stations". 48 m range practice.	
"	20.		Parades under Coy Commanders. Instructional classes continued. Reconnaissance of AUBOIRES - HAVERSKERQUE line by Officers and N.C.O's	
"	21	7:30 AM 7. P.M.	Holy Communion. Voluntary Evening service at Recreational games under Coy Commanders.	
"	22		Parades under Coy Commanders. Recreational Instructional classes continued. Lewis gun range practice.	

R.L. Haynes adjt Lt Col
Commanding 12 (W.S.) B'n. S.L.I.

Army Form C. 2118.

WAR DIARY
or
INTELLIGENCE SUMMARY.

(Erase heading not required.) 12th (West Somerset Yeomanry) Bn Somerset LI

Place	Date	Hour	Summary of Events and Information	Remarks and references to Appendices
Pk Moh Trace Sheet 36a A700 LA MIQUELLERIE (036a)	July 23.		"B" Team and supernumeraries marched to the Divisional Reception at N14.c.2.6. The Transport and Administrative portion of the Bn to MOLINGHEM. At 8.P.M. the Bn moved from billets to relieve the 15th SUFFOLK Bn in the line. "C" Coy taking over the front line Q14.c and 20 to forming their own supports. "A" Coy taking over the right Reserve sector in Q19.d, "D" Coy taking over the Left Reserve sector in Q19.a, Bn HQ at CARVIN (P2 & 8.7) B Coy going into the AMUSORIES – HAVERSKERQUE. The relief was completed by 12.30.A.M.	
	24.		Front line "C" Coy from Q20.b.3.9 to Q14.c.5.9. Reserve Companies (AdD) from Q19.d.3.8 to Q13.c.4.9. "B" Coy in the AMUSORIES – HAVERSKERQUE line. Enemy artillery activity above normal. L.F.E.A. NIL. Gas shells NIL. 1 Off. 2.O.R. left Q14.c.9.4 at 11.30 PM to ascertain strength of enemy post Q14.d.0.7 and if possible to deal with it. Post held by 9 men and a light M.G. apparently no surprise in front of it. The whole patrol became casualties but returned via Q14.c9.4 at 12.45 A.M. Commanding 12(W.S.Y) Bn S.L.I.	

WAR DIARY
INTELLIGENCE SUMMARY

Army Form C. 2118.

(Erase heading not required) 1/2th (West Somerset Yeomanry) Bn Somerset L.I.

Place	Date July	Hour	Summary of Events and Information	Remarks and references to Appendices.
Ref Map Sheet 36a 1/40,000 France	24		(Continued) A second patrol of 3. O.R. reconnoitred enemy's defences from Q14.b.8.1 at 3:20 A.M. via Q14.b.8.1 to Q14.d.2.5. Wire along enemy's front was lit and thick. Corn has not been cut in front of wire. M.G. were located at Q14.d.9.1. Q14.d.7.5. Q14.b.6.3. Q14.d.2.7.5. Casualties during day nil :- Wounded Capt E.F.S. RODD. 2Lt. B.L. HADDON and 5. O.R. Disposition of Bn as for 24th. Enemy artillery above normal. F.E.A. 50 Blue and Yellow Cross gas shells on Q20.a.d.c. Listening Posts at Q14.d.7.2.J did not locate or hear any of the enemy. L.F.E.A. active during the night 25-26. Casualties two O.R. killed :- 5. O.R. wounded.	
"	25			
"	26		Disposition as for 24th. Increased enemy artillery activity. L.F.E.A. two at about 9. A.M. Gas shells NIL. Casualties NIL.	
"	27		Disposition as for 24th. Enemy artillery less active. L.F.E.A. NIL. Gas shells. NIL. at 11 P.M. to "Ascertain if any enemy movement from Q20.b.93 enemy machine gun was firing from home in Q14.d.3.8. No tracks leading through wire in front of hazel. No enemy seen or heard Major C.R. Hayward. No movement of troops seen a heard Major C.R. Hayward. Commanding 12 (W.S.Y.) Bn SLI	

E.W. Hayward Major Lt Col.
Commanding 12(W.S.Y.)Bn S.L.I

WAR DIARY
INTELLIGENCE SUMMARY

(Erase heading not required). 1/2 (WSy) Bn Somerset Light Infantry

Place	Date July	Hour	Summary of Events and Information	Remarks and references to Appendices.
Ref Map sheet 36cu 1/10,000 France	28		Dispositions of Bn as for 27th. Hostile artillery normal. T.M. one firing from Q11c20. L.F.E.A. NIL. Gas shelling NIL. Patrol of 4 O.R. left Q11c105 at 10.30 P.M. to reconnoitre enemy dispositions in Q11d28. A.M. Gun was located in house in Q11d38. M.G. located Q11d18. Enemy not holding work in field Q11d28 with increased numbers, about 15. Hedge Q11d18 & Q11d27 is now wired up. Enemy now very much alert in this vicinity.	
	29		Dispositions of Bn as for 24th. Hostile Artillery more active than usual. T.M. firing from Q15c20. L.F.E.A. NIL. Gas shelling NIL. Patrol of 1 off 3 O.R. left Q20b29 at 9.50 P.M. to proceed to shell holes Q11d83. If held to ascertain number and if possible deal with them. Found shell holes unoccupied searched all shell holes in vicinity which showed no trace of occupation. Then proceeded to rest of shell holes in Q11d6535 and found them also unoccupied. Located M.G. firing from house in Q11d38. Considerable enemy movement heard between house Q11d38 and house Q11d6575. No tracks were found leading from enemy wire.	

E.P. Waggoner ?
Lt Col.
Commanding 1/2 (WSy) Bn S.L.I.

Army Form C. 2118.

WAR DIARY
or
INTELLIGENCE SUMMARY.

(Erase heading not required). 12th (West Somerset Yeo) Bn Somerset L.I.

Place	Date	Hour	Summary of Events and Information	Remarks and references to Appendices.
Ref Map France Sheet 36a 1/5000	30		Disposition of Bn. as for 24th. Hostile artillery very active. L.F.E.A. one about 8 A.M. Hostile artillery very active about 9.30 P.M. at Q.19 central. Patrol of 1 Off. 6. O.R. left Q.20 b.8.3 at 9.45 P.M. to proceed to Q.14.d.8.5.2.0, ascertain strength of garrison and if possible deal with it. Patrol proceeded to Q.14.d.8.5.20 enemy patrol heard passing our patrol about Q.14.d.4.1. Our patrol halted and tried to locate enemy patrol but the high corn rendered this impossible. M.G. emplacements located in shell hole at Q.14 d 6.1. Working parties located Q.14 d 8.5.20. After repairing our wires a L.G. was turned on the working party.	
	31		Disposition of Bn as for 24th. Hostile artillery active about 8.30 A.M. to 9 A.M. about 20 5.9 dropping around Bn HQ. L.F.E.A. NIL. Quiet day on the whole. The Bn was relieved at 12 midnight by the 14th R.H. and marched into Bde Reserve at LA PIERRIERE. The relief was carried out quite quietly without casualties.	

C.H. Haywood
Major
Commanding 12(WSy) Bn S.L.I.

HQ. 229 Bde

Herewith War Diary for month of August.

Delay regretted.

6/9/18

R T Dommett
FEW1

229/74 Army Form C. 2118.

WAR DIARY
INTELLIGENCE SUMMARY

(Erase heading not required). 12th (West Somerset Yeomanry) Bn. Som. L.I.

Vol 5

Place	Date	Hour	Summary of Events and Information	Remarks and references to Appendices.
Ref Map France Sheet 36	August 1918			
	1.		Bn in Bde Reserve in billets at LA PIERRIERE. Working party of 4 Off. 200.OR sent to work in Reserve line, parading at 3/5AM. Officers and NCOs reconnoitred the routes & dispositions as laid down in 229 Bde Reserve Bn Defence Scheme, returning at 8.P.M.	
	2.		Bn in Bde Reserve in billets at LA PIERRIERE. 1 Off. 50.OR working party on new Bn HQ at P23 d88 from 8AM to 4.PM. 3 Off. 200.OR working party on Reserve Line 9.30PM to 3.AM. Officers and NCOs reconnoitred routes and dispositions as laid down in 229 Bde Reserve Bn Defence Scheme.	
	3.		Bn in Bde Reserve at LA PIERRIERE. 1 Off. 50.OR work at P23 d 3.8 from 8AM to 4.PM. 3 Off. and 200.OR working party on Reserve Line 9.30PM to 3.AM. A & C Coy had use of baths at GUARBECQUE.	
	4.		Bn in Bde Reserve at LA PIERRIERE. Holy Communion at 9 A.M. Voluntary Service at 6.30.PM. (National Day of Prayer). Working party of 1 Off & 50.OR at P23 d 3.8 from 8AM to 4.PM. Working party of 3 Off. 200.OR on the Reserve Line from 9.30.PM.	

C. M. Drummond Major
Commanding 12th (W.Sy) Bn S.L.I.

Army Form C. 2118.

WAR DIARY
or
INTELLIGENCE SUMMARY.

(Erase heading not required). 12th (West Somerset Yeo) Bn Som. L.I.

Place	Date	Hour	Summary of Events and Information	Remarks and references to Appendices.
Ref Map France Sheet 36a SE			August 1918.	
	5.		Bn in Bde Reserve at LA PIERRIERE. Working party of 1 Off and 50 OR at P23 d 8.4 from 8 A.M. to 4 P.M. 3 officers and 200 OR working party on Reserve line from 9.30 PM to 3 A.M. Casualties 4 OR wounded.	
	6.		Bn in Bde Reserve at LA PIERRIERE. Working party of 1 Off & 50 OR at P23 d 8.4 from 8 A.M. to 4 P.M. and 3 officers and 200 OR worked on Reserve line from 9.30 PM to 3 A.M. Bde coy JHQ had use of baths at GUARBECQUE.	
	7.		Bn in Bde Reserve at LA PIERRIERE. Working party of 1 Off & 50 OR at P23 d 8.4 from 8 AM until withdrawn. At 1.P.M Bn received orders to move forward on account of the front line being advanced. The Bn marched forward at 2.30 P.M to Bn JHQ P23 d 8.4. A Coy to the Reserve line & AMUSOIRES line. B & C Coys in the AMUSOIRES line at P29 b & d P30 a&c. D Coy to frontline & the AMUSOIRES line P23 b & d.	
	8.		At 10. A.M the Bn moved forward to relieve the 11th Devons The Bn. relief completed by 1.30 P.M. Disposition of Bn from right to left. Front line D & B Coy from Q9 d 3.7 to Q9 a 3.5. A Coy in support from Q8 c 2.2 to Q8 a 3.2. C Coy in Reserve. Bn Reserve at from Q13 c 3.7 to Q9 d 5.9 Bn HQ Q7 d 50.45.	

G.H. Heywood Major
Commanding 12 (W.Sy) Bn. S.L.I

WAR DIARY
INTELLIGENCE SUMMARY

12th (WEST SOMERSET YEO) Bn Som L.I.

Place	Date	Hour	Summary of Events and Information	Remarks and references to Appendices.
Ref Map FRANCE Sheets 36 a SE 1/20,000	8 August 1918	(Continued)	At 5.30 P.M. orders were received from Bde that the line would advance at 6. P.M. The artillery bombarded from 5.30 to 6 P.M. the objective being given as the COURANT de TURBEAUTÉ in Q4 a 5.5 to Q.10 b 1.3. At 6. P.M. B&D Coys moved forward & very little resistance was met with until reaching the track running N.W. through Q. 10 c and a, when very heavy machine gun fire was experienced chiefly from the left flank, the objective was gained at 8. P.M. and consolidated immediately. During the advance all the Officers C.S.M. and 3 Sergts of D Coy became casualties, 395088 Sergt. E.J. WARFIELD, quickly grasped the situation, took command, led the Coy on to the final objective and at once sent a most valuable report back to the Bn Commander. Two platoons under 2Lt Hewitt were sent to the right from C Coy from the Support (A Coy) the remainder moving up to where the firing line was, prior to the advance. Casualties: Killed 8. OR. Wounded. Capt A.H. WHEELER, M.C. 2Lt T.S. PRICE. And 24. OR.	

C.H. Wayman
Major
Commanding 12th (W Sy) Bn. S.L.I.

Army Form C. 2118.

WAR DIARY
or
INTELLIGENCE SUMMARY

(Erase heading not required). 12th (West Som't Yeo) Bn Som't L.I.

Place	Date	Hour	Summary of Events and Information	Remarks and references to Appendices.
Mont Kokt FRANCE Sh 57d.S.E —57500	9.		August 1918. Small patrols were pushed out continually throughout the day as failure to ascertain disposition and strength of enemy in front. It was found that the enemy held a trench system running N.W. through a5c & 84y patched with wire. Disposition of Bn D&B Coys Q10d.1.3.6. HQ.4 a 5.5 also hd qtrs of A. Coy Q9d.3.7.16 0 Q9e 80.95. E coy Q13c.3.7.6 Q7d 5.9. Bn HQ Q7d 50.75. LFEA two at 5:15AM and 8PM. At 8:30 PM. A coy relieved D coy from the front line. D coy coming back into Support. Enemy artillery active throughout the day. Casualties 2 OR. wounded.	
	10		Disposition of Bn as for 9th. enemy artillery very active throughout the day especially on the Support line. Patrols sent out continually but found enemy in strength opposite them with forward machine gun posts. LFEA 7 dead enemy were found out the Bn front and identifications taken. At 12 mid - night the Bn was relieved by the 16th Suffolk Bn 230 Bde marching back to positions in the AMUSORIES – HAVERSKERQUE line. Casualties wounded 2LC Hewitt and 7. OR.	

C.V.Maynard
Major.
Commanding 12(W.Sy)Bn S.L.I.

WAR DIARY
INTELLIGENCE SUMMARY

Army Form C. 2118.

Place	Date	Hour	Summary of Events and Information	Remarks and references to Appendices.
Mof up FRANCE Sheet 36a SE 1/20000	August 1918			
	11		Disposition of Bn. "A" Coy old reserve line Q19d. "B" Coy AMUSOIRIES line P30a&b. "C" Coy old reserve line P19a and 13c. "D" Coy AMUSORIES line P23d and b. Bn HQ P23d 80.45. Casualties 2 O.R. wounded	
"	12.		Disposition of Bn as for 11th inst. Working party of 4 officers & 100 O.R. under R.E's at work on reserve line. Working party of 1 Off. and 50. O.R. at P23d 8.4. Casualties killed 5. O.R. wounded 4. O.R.	
"	13.		Disposition of Bn as for 11th inst. Working party of 1 officer and 50. O.R. from 8.A.M. to 4 P.M at P23d 8.4. Working party of two officers and 50.O.R. wiring in front of Reserve trenches. Casualties 1. O.R. wounded.	
"	14		Disposition of Bn as for 11th inst. Working party of 1 officer and 50. O.R. from 8.A.M. until task completed at P23d 8.4. Working party of 1 officer and 60.O.R. harvesting corn crops. 100 O.R. worked for 3 hours in front of the Reserve line hitting up wire.	

E.M. Weymouth
Major
Commanding 12(W.S⁴)Bn S.L.I

Army Form C. 2118.

WAR DIARY
or
INTELLIGENCE SUMMARY.

(Erase heading not required). 12th (West Somerset Yeomanry) Bn. Som. L.I.

Place	Date	Hour	Summary of Events and Information	Remarks and references to Appendices.
Ref. Map Sheet 36a FRANCE 1/40,000	15.		August 1918. Disposition of Bn. as for 11th inst. Working party of 1 Off. and 50 OR at P23d 8.4 from 8.A.M. until task completed. 1 Off. and 60 OR working party harvesting corn crops. 3 Officers and 150 OR put up 500 yds of apron wire fence in front of Reserve Line.	
—	16.		Disposition of Bn. as for 11th inst. Working party of 1 Off. and 50 OR at P23d 8.4 from 8.A.M. until task completed. 1 Off. and 60 OR working at harvesting corn crops. At 9.45 P.M. the Bn. was relieved by the 15th Suffolk Bn., and marched to billets at GUARBECQUE.	
GUARBECQUE	17		Billeted at GUARBECQUE. Parades under Coy Commanders.	
	18		200 OR has use of baths at GUARBECQUE. Bde Church Parade Service at O28d 3.8. at which the Army Commander Genl. Sir W.R.BIRDWOOD. K.C.B. K.C.M.G. &c. was present. After the Service the Bde marched past by Platoons. Voluntary Service at 5.15 P.M.	

C.V.Heyward
Major
Commanding 12 (W.S.Y.) Bn. S.L.I.

Army Form C. 2118.

WAR DIARY
or
INTELLIGENCE SUMMARY

12th (West Somerset Yeo.) Bn Som. L.I.

(Erase heading not required.)

Instructions regarding War Diaries and Intelligence Summaries are contained in F.S. Regs., Part II. and the Staff Manual respectively. Title pages will be prepared in manuscript.

Place	Date	Hour	Summary of Events and Information	Remarks and references to Appendices.
Ref Map. FRANCE Sheet 36a 1/10,000 GUARBECQUE	August 1918. 19.		Billeted at GUARBECQUE. 3 Officers and OR 200 haversting in the back area. Signallers, Scouts, Lewis Gun, & Wiring classes commenced. Parades under Coy Commanders.	
GUARBECQUE	20.		Billets at GUARBECQUE. The Bn was inspected by Lt. Genl. Sir. R.C.B. HAKING. K.C.B. KCM.G etc. by the Corps Commander. A Coy & HQ at 10.A.M. Afternoon parades commencing with Transport. Instructional Classes continued.	
GUARBECQUE	21		Parades under Company Commanders. Instructional Classes continued. Bathing parades.	
	22		Parades under Company Commanders. Instructional Classes continued. 1 Officer and 50 OR haversting party under the Divisional Agricultural Officer. 2.30 PM Water Sports were held in the LA BASSEE CANAL.	

C.N. Maywaring Major
Commanding 12 (WSY) Bn Som. L.I.

WAR DIARY
INTELLIGENCE SUMMARY

(Erase heading not required.) 12th (West Somerset Yeomanry) Bn Som L I

Army Form C. 2118.

Place	Date	Hour	Summary of Events and Information	Remarks and references to Appendices.
R/Map FRANCE Sheet 36a 1:40000.			August 1918	
	23		Billeted at GUARBECQUE. Parades under Company Commanders. Instructional Classes continued. C.O. and Coy Commrs reconnoitred the line held by the 24th Bn WELSH Regt. Announced in Corps Routine Orders that Pte. BAKER & BEER had been awarded with the Military Medal for "gallantry in action" as stretcher bearers. Lt. Stephens to Divisional Reception Camp as Adjutant.	
	24		At 8.AM the Bn marched out of billets at GUARBECQUE reaching ROBECQUE at 10.AM. Preparatory to taking over the line held by the 24th Bn WELSH REGT. At 9.15.P.M. the Bn moved forward and relieved the above Bn, relief completed by 1.35.AM. All four Companies in the line with two platoons in the front line and two platoons each in Support. Disposition of Bn. A Coy from R7C0.7 to R13a.3.7. Coy HQ Q12c.3.7. B Coy R13a.3.7 to R13c.6.4 Coy HQ Q18c.1.7. "C" Coy R13c.7.4 to R19 ? 1.3 Coy HQ Q18c.8.0. D Coy R19t.1.2 to R19d 10.0. Aid Post Q22a.2.1. Bn HQ. Q16d.7.3.	
	25			

C.V. Weguere
Major.
Commanding 12(WSY) Bn Som L.I.

WAR DIARY
or
INTELLIGENCE SUMMARY.

(Erase heading not required). 12(W.S.Y)Bn Som L.I.

Army Form C. 2118.

Place	Date	Hour	Summary of Events and Information	Remarks and references to Appendices.
Ref. Map. FRANCE. Sheet 36a	26		Disposition of Bn as for 25th. 4 patrols were sent out during the 24 hours, no enemy encountered, 3 machine guns located and artillery informed. Enemy machine guns active. Enemy artillery active especially on front and support lines. After Blue, Green and Yellow Cross shells. Casualties 1 O.R. wounded, 2 O.R. missing believed prisoners of war.	
	27.		Disposition of Bn as for 25th. 7 patrols were sent out during the 24 hours. One enemy patrol (7.OR) encountered they hastily with- drew. 5 M.G. and 2 T.M. located, artillery informed. Enemy M.G. active. Enemy artillery normal. After Blue and Green Cross shells. Enemy knocked out main Bn. observation post. Casualties 1 O.R. killed. Bn was relieved by the 11th Bn Somerset L.I. relief completed at 1.45 A.M.	
MANQUEVILLE	28.		Billeted at MANQUEVILLE. On relief the Bn marched to ROBECQUE, there entrusing for MANQUEVILLE arriving at 5.15 A.M.	

C.V.Dayman
Major
Commanding 12th(W.S.Y)Bn Som L.I.

Army Form C. 2118.

WAR DIARY
~~INTELLIGENCE SUMMARY~~

(Erase heading not required). 12th (West-Somerset Yeo) Bn Somt L.I.

Instructions regarding War Diaries and Intelligence Summaries are contained in F.S. Regs., Part II. and the Staff Manual respectively. Title pages will be prepared in manuscript.

Place	Date	Hour	Summary of Events and Information	Remarks and references to Appendices.
Maj Rol France Sheet 53a 14.50.00 / AMIENS. 17. 1.50.00.	August 1918. 29.		Battalion paraded at 3.A.M. marched to BURGUETTE STATION entrained at 10. A.M. en route for CORBIE.	
	30.		Arrived at CORBIE at about 2.A.M. detrained and marched off at 4.A.M. reaching FRANVILLERS at 6.50 A.M. going into billets. All surplus Stores and kits dumped. "B" team detailed.	
	31.		Billets at FRANVILLERS. 1.30 P.M. received orders to despatch "B" Team remainder of Bn to endeavors at 2.30 P.M. Detrained at about 8.P.M. at A4ult 51 and marched to MARICOURT where packs and great coats were dumped, thence to bivouac in South of LE FOREST.	

E.J. Weymouth
Major.
Commanding 12 (W.S.Y.) Bn Somt L.I.

A.P. & S.D., Alex./2000/11:17/5M. W.M. & Co.

WAR DIARY
or
INTELLIGENCE SUMMARY

Army Form C. 2118.

(Erase heading not required.) 12th (West Somerset Yeomanry) Bn Som L.I.

Place	Date	Hour	Summary of Events and Information	Remarks and references to Appendices.
MAP REF FRANCE Sheet 62c NW	Sept 1st 1918		Bivouac South of LE FOREST. (B.16) Moved out to relieve the 41st and 42nd Bns A.I.F. on line C.31.d.4.0 to C.18.6.10, relief completed by 11:49 P.M.	
	2	12:30 A.M.	Line moved forward and took up battle outpost. At 5:15 A.M. the barrage opened, the attack commenced, the barrage creeping forward at the rate of 100 yds in 5 minutes. The Bde attacked on a two Bn frontage, 10th S.L.I. on right, 14th R.H. on left, 12th Devons in Support. The Bn attacked on a two company frontage A Coy on the right & Coy on the left B and D Coys in close Support. The attack was met with heavy resistance from the enemy, Artillery and machine gun fire being exceptionally severe. In spite of heavy casualties the advance was carried forward until across the CANAL DU NORD South of MOISLAINS, when the enemy put in a strong counter attack which came in front also on the flank from MOISLAINS, which held up the advance, the counter attack was eventually driven off. Severe M.G. fire was experienced from the village of HAUT ALLAINES, and the village had to be dealt with both the Bn out off the direction of the advance. The line was reorganised at C29c and the advance continued until the line C34d.5.0 to C.24.b.3.0 was reached, when the order was given to withdraw to the SCUTARI - BROUSSA Trenches in C.23.a and C.22.c. The withdraw was effected in good order and practically without casualties. After the	

E.W. Dugmore Major
Commanding 12 (W.S.Y.) Bn S.L.I.

Army Form C. 2118.

WAR DIARY
or
INTELLIGENCE SUMMARY.

(Erase heading not required). 12th (West Somerset Yeomanry) Bn Somt L.I.

Instructions regarding War Diaries and Intelligence Summaries are contained in F.S. Regs., Part II. and the Staff Manual respectively. Title pages will be prepared in manuscript.

Place	Date	Hour	Summary of Events and Information	Remarks and references to Appendices.
REF MAP FRANCE Sheet 62c. NW 1/20000	September 1918		SCUTARI & BROUSSA Trenches were reached they were subjected to heavy shell fire, (H.E. Shrapnel & Gas) from the enemy artillery but the line was easily held. Casualties Killed. Capt. T.F. WALLIS. Wounded. Capt. W.A. KEEN. Lieut. D.B. TAYLOR. Lieut. J.W. HARTNELL. 2Lt. WILLS. " E.G. THOMSON. " J.B. CLARKE. 2Lt. W.H. FIRMAN " JENKINS. " J.P.D. VALLOW " PIPER. Other ranks. Killed. 41. Wounded 161. Missing 14. An extraordinary large number of dead enemy were accounted for.	
"	3-		Held line in BROUSSA TRENCH from C.32.a.9.0 to C.16.d.3.0. at 10.PM the line was advanced.	
"	4		3.30.A.M. new line was established from C.30.c.5.8 to C.24.c.7.8. 'A' Coy on right. D Coy on left back being joined with the 14th R.H. on left & Australians on right. B&C Coy in Support from C.29.8.5.2 to C.23.d.9.9. Relieved at 11 PM by the 15th Suffolks & 11th Bn.s marched to bivouac in B.30.b.	
"	5		Bivouac B.30 & B.8. Burial parties sent out. Salvage continued. Reorganizing and equipping.	

C.W. Haymand Major

Commanding 12th (W.S.Y) Bn Somt L.I.

Army Form C. 2118.

WAR DIARY
or
INTELLIGENCE SUMMARY

(Erase heading not required) 13 (West Somerset Yeomanry) Bn Som: L.I.

Place	Date	Hour	Summary of Events and Information	Remarks and references to Appendices.
Map Ref. FRANCE Sheet 62c N.W.	September 1918.			
	6		Bivouac at B30 & 8.8. Burial and salvaging parties sent out. 5.30 P.M. marched to bivouac area near AIZECOURT (J.1 & central).	
Spreegnes	7		Bivouac at (J1 & central). B.O.C. had conference and briefed to all officers at 11.30 A.M. Instructional classes continued. Parades and Coy Commrs. Moved out at 3 P.M. marched to LONGAVESNES occupied trenches from K1&8.5 to E26C10 Bn HQ E25A7.0. Disposition of Bn as for 9th inst. Officers went on a reconnaissance forward. 11.15 P.M. marched out to relieve 231st Bde.	
"	8			
"	9		Relieved K.S.L.I. at 3.30 A.M. Devons on right. R.H. on left. 1/2 H.S.L.I. on D. Coy in Reserve. Disposition of Bn. D. Coy attached to 14 Royal Highlanders in line from F25 b2.6 to F19 d2.5. A Coy E23 d6.2 to E23 d6.7. B&C. Coys. E30 a2.0 to E30 a5.9. Bn. HQ E29 b3.6.	
"	10		Disposition of Bn as for 9th inst. At 5.30 A.M. B. de attached "D" Coy (under orders 14th R.H.) in the centre, the line reached (approx) F26 a2.9 to F20 e9.3, when a very strong	

E.M. Daywaring Major
Commanding 1/3th (W.Sy) Bn. S.L.I.

Army Form C. 2118.

WAR DIARY
or
~~INTELLIGENCE SUMMARY.~~
(Erase heading not required). 12th (West Somerset Yeomanry) Bn Som L.I.

Place	Date	Hour	Summary of Events and Information	Remarks and references to Appendices.
TEMPLEUX LE FOSSE	September 1918			
	10 (continued)		enemy counter attack was met with, & drove in the right front line. Casualties: found the line to withdraw to the original front line. Casualties wounded O.R. 12. Missing Capt F.F. Edmonton, M.C. and 2/Lt O.R. At 11 P.M. the Bn was relieved by the 230th Bde; the 1/5 Suffolk Rgmt taking over from this Bn.	
	11		On relief by the Suffolk Rgmt the Bn marched to a bivouac area near TEMPLEUX-LE-FOSSE, arriving about 4:30 A.M.	
	12		Bde in Divisional Reserve. Bn at J6C (near TEMPLEUX-LE-FOSSE) Parades under Coy Commanders. Instructional classes continued. Lts YANDLE and WARREN also 2Lts FERRIS & FELLOWS, joined the Battalion.	
	13		In bivouac near TEMPLEUX-LE-FOSSE J.6.C. Parades under Company Commanders. Instructional classes continued. The Commanding Officer inspected the B. Coys. L. G. class had use of 30 yds range.	

E.J. Wayman, Major
Commanding 12 (W.S.Y.) Bn Som L.I.

Army Form C. 2118.

WAR DIARY
or
INTELLIGENCE SUMMARY

(Erase heading not required). 12th (West Somerset Yeomanry) Bn Somt L.I.

Place	Date	Hour	Summary of Events and Information	Remarks and references to Appendices.
Ref Map. FRANCE. Sheet 62c NE. 1/20,000	14		In bivouac near TEMPLEUX-le-FOSSÉ. T.6.c. Parades under Company Commanders. Instructional classes continued. L.G. class had use of 30 yds range. The C.O. inspected C & D. Coys.	
	15		In bivouac near TEMPLEUX-le-FOSSÉ. T.6.c. Parades under Company Commanders. Instructional classes continued. The C.O. inspected A Coy. Square J 5 a 8 cleared of salvage.	
	16		Bivouac near TEMPLEUX-le-FOSSÉ. T.6.c. Parades under Coy Commanders. Squares J. 5.11. & 12 cleared of all salvage. At 7.30.P.M. marched forward to bivouac A Coy. E29 q b 3 1. B Coy E29 q b 3 4. C&D Coys. E29 q 6 6 7. Bn HQ SPUR QUARRY.	
	17		Came under orders of 236th Bde. From 1 to 5.30.AM. heavily bombarded by Yellow Cross gas shells and H.E. during this time and in spite of every precaution and the moving of the troops few casualties were caused. Disposition of Bn. A Coy. E29 q b 3 1. B Coy. E29 q b 3 4. C&D Coys E29 q b 6 7. Bn HQ SPUR QUARRY E29 c 8 7.	

E.V. Whyward Major
Commanding 12th Somt L.I.

WAR DIARY
or
INTELLIGENCE SUMMARY

Army Form C. 2118.

12th (West Somerset Yeomanry) Bn Som. L.I.

Place	Date	Hour	Summary of Events and Information	Remarks and references to Appendices.
RUMA FRANCE SHEET 51 B	September 1918		Attack by 230 Bde and 231 reinforced by 13 on each of the 229 Bde Somersets & 230 Bde Devons to 231 Bde. The 230 Bde attacked on a two Bn frontage the Suffolks on right Sussex on left led the attack and captured the Green line L14.c.9.0, L43.d.4.6, F28.b.2.0, Connor Post, Toine Post and continuation of French system North, East, & South. Le Bn Boundary L1.a.0.8, L3.b.10.8, F25.c.0.0, F39.a.0.0 – thence due East. The Buffs on right Somersets on left followed the attack passing through the Suffolks and Sussex respectively on the given line, continued the advance, captured and consolidated the RED LINE A25.d.3.0, F30.e.1.8, F30.e.3.7, Rifleman Post, Benjamin Post etc. The attack was carried out under a moving barrage. Zero hour went 5.40 AM. Owing to the Bn being so weak in strength it was reinforced by "A" Coy 14 Royal Highlanders. A B C & D Coys led with He IIIICH in close support role in inforce the leading line or He Disposition of 2 R front line F29.1.10.9, E. Benjamin Post, Bn HQ F28.d.1.1. Casualties Killed 4 O.R., Wounded Capt SPINITTALL and 46. O.R. Prisoners captured unwounded 3 offs. 62. O.R. wounded 1 off. 12. O.R.	

C.V. Hayward Major
Commanding 1/2 Som. L.I.

WAR DIARY
INTELLIGENCE SUMMARY

12th (West Somerset Yeo) Bn Som L.I.

Army Form C. 2118.

Place	Date	Hour	Summary of Events and Information	Remarks and references to Appendices.
Map Ref. FRANCE Sherbrene 1/20000	September 1918. 19.		Disposition of Bn front line from F.29.d.10.9 to BENJAMIN POST. Bn HQ F.28.d.1.1. Enemy artillery active throughout the day, at 10.15AM and 4.30.P.M. he put down a barrage on the front line and between the front line and Bn HQ. LFEA two at 4.P.M. casualties wounded 4 OR. The Bn was relieved by the Sussex Bn at 11 P.M.	
	20		After relief marched to bivouac area near ROISEL occupying huts of an old POW compound. At 4.30.P.M. received orders that the 229 Bde would support the 230 & 231 Bdes in an attack on the "Blue line" (A36d central – QUINNEMONT PIT LANE) the following day. At 9.30 P.M. marched forward and occupied TEMPLEUX QUARRY. Casualties 2. OR. wounded. Bivouac in TEMPLEUX QUARRY, moved out and occupied green line at 1.30. P.M. Disposition of Bn. A&B Coys TOINE POST C&D Coys. CONNOR POST. Bn HQ F.28.d.1.1. At 11.35.P.M. draft of 2 Lt. RICHARDS and 137. OR. arrived and posted to Coys.	

C.R. Waymouth
Major
Commanding 12 (W.S.Y) Bn. S.L.I.

WAR DIARY
or
INTELLIGENCE SUMMARY.
(Erase heading not required.)

Army Form C. 2118.

Place	Date	Hour	Summary of Events and Information	Remarks and references to Appendices
Ref Map FRANCE. Sheet 62NE. 1/20000			September 1918.	
	22		Disposition as for 21st. Moved forward at 10 P.M. in support to the front line Companies lining HUSSAR ROAD from right F.29.d.6.4 to left F.23.c.2.4 in the order of B.A & D Coys. forward Command Post at F.29.6.0.5. Bn H.Q.F.28.d.1.1. Casualties Killed Lieut C.G. THOMSON. wounded 4. O.R. O.C. 14.R.H. and 16th Devons each had a call on one of the Coys in support without reference to the Commanding Officer.	
	23		Disposition on HUSSAR ROAD as for 22nd. Casualties wounded 2 Lt A.E. PERRY 3rd Som L.I. and 4. O.R.	
	24		Disposition on HUSSAR ROAD as for 22nd. At 11:30 P.M. the Bn was relieved by the 106th Bn. United States Army. When relief the Bn marched to linquae area near ROISEL (K.16.).	
	25. 9.		Marched to TINCOURT Station where B Team and re-enforcements (5 off & 122 OR) joined the Bn. Entrained at 3.45 P.M. arriving at VILLERS BRETONNEUX at 4.30 P.M. and marched to billets at CORBIE	

E.M. Maynard Major.
Commanding 12th Som L.I.

Army Form C. 2118.

WAR DIARY
~~INTELLIGENCE SUMMARY~~

(Erase heading not required.) 12th (West Somerset Yeomanry) Bn Som L.I.

Instructions regarding War Diaries and Intelligence Summaries are contained in F.S. Regs., Part II. and the Staff Manual respectively. Title pages will be prepared in manuscript.

Place	Date	Hour	Summary of Events and Information	Remarks and references to Appendices
Ref Map Sheet 62.e 1/40,000			September 1918.	
	26		Billets at CORBIE. Draft of 91 O.R. arrived. Parade under Coy Commanders. The C.O. inspected the drafts at 2 P.M. Lt.Col. G.S. POOLE. D.S.O. resumed command of the Battalion.	
	27		Billets at CORBIE. Parade under Coy Commdrs. Paraded at 4.30 P.M. and marched to MERICOURT-L'ABBÉ, bivouaching for the night near the station.	
	28		Entrained at MERICOURT station at 6 A.M. Detrained at BERGUETTE station at 5 P.M. and marched to billets at MANQUEVILLE.	
	29		Parade under Coy Commdrs. Holy Communion at 11.30 A.M. Capt. H. FORREST. R.A.M.C. To Hosp. Lieut. A.J. MEEK. posted to Bn as medical officer.	

			Lieut R.L. SCUBBY. 2Lt. W.E. PARKER. Willis Regiment joined the Battalion
			2Lt. C.E. PEARCE. " F.E. SPOKES.
			  " E.R. COWAN. " A.H.B. BISHOP.
			  " L.J. MARSH. " H.T. McLACHLAN.
			  " C.B. KERSLAKE. " E.R. HUMPHRIS.
			  " F.R. SHARMAN.	

G. Poole
Lt Col
Commanding 12th = S.L.I.

Army Form C. 2118.

WAR DIARY
or
INTELLIGENCE SUMMARY

(Erase heading not required.) 12th (West Somerset Yeo) Bn Somt L.I.

Place	Date	Hour	Summary of Events and Information	Remarks and references to Appendices
Ref Map Sheet 36a 1/40,000	September 1918.			
	30.		Billets at MANQUEVILLE. Parades under Company Commanders. Signallers, Lewis Gunners & Scouts Instructional Classes. Lt YANDLE, 2Lt FERRIS to hospital.	

E.P. Poole
Lt Col.
Commanding 12th (W.Sy) Bn Somt L.I.

HQ 229th Infty Bde.

Herewith War Diary for this Bn for month of September.

1/10/18

R. T. Domnett Capt.
For O.C. 12th S.L.I.

WAR DIARY

Army Form C. 2118.

12th (West Somt. Yeo.) Bn Somt. L.I.

INTELLIGENCE SUMMARY

Place	Date	Hour	Summary of Events and Information	Remarks and references to Appendices
FRANCE Sheet 36a	October 1918.			
	1.		Billets at MANQUEVILLE. Parades under Coy Commanders. Instructional classes continued.	
	2.		Billets at MANQUEVILLE. Parades under Coy Commanders. Instructional classes continued. 1100 marched BURBURE and entrained on light railway, detained at ESSAIRS and marched to billets relieving KSLI 231st Bde. Draft of 41 OR arrived.	
Sheet 36 S.W.	3.		Billets at ESSAIRS. Parades under Coy Commanders. Instructional classes continued. At 1515 received orders to move forward. 1430 marched to Bivouac Square S 4.5.10.14. Bn HQ S9 b.2.7.	
	4.		0800 marched to billets in HERLIES (T&d). Bn HQ T&d 5.0.	
	5.		Billets at HERLIES (T&d). Bn HQ T&d 5.0. Parades under Coy Commanders. Instructional classes continued. Major C.R. HAYWARD to England for course.	

E.M. Boyle
Lt-Col.
Commanding 12th (W.S.Y.) Bn. S.L.I.

WAR DIARY
INTELLIGENCE SUMMARY

(Erase heading not required.) 12th (West Somerset Yeomanry) Bn Som L.I.

Army Form C. 2118.

Place	Date	Hour	Summary of Events and Information	Remarks and references to Appendices
Mat Ref FRANCE Sheet 36.S.W.6	October 1918		Billets at HERLIES (T.H.d) Bn HQ T4d 5.0. Parades under Company Commanders, Instructional classes continued. Lieut W.C. CROSS D.C.M rejoined from hospital.	
			Draft of 89 joined Bn from 3rd Somt L.I.	
	7		Billets at HERLIES (T.H.d) Bn HQ T4d 5.0. Parades under Company Commanders, Instructional classes continued. 2 Lt MATEER rejoined from hospital.	
	8		Billets at HERLIES (T.H.d) Bn HQ T4d 5.0. Parades under Company Commanders, Instructional classes continued. The Commanding Officers inspected the draft. Reconnaissance made of the line held by the 231st Infa Bde with a view to taking over.	
	9		Billets at HERLIES (T.H.d) Bn HQ T4d 5.0. Parades under Company Commanders, Instructional classes continued	

G.A. Poole
Lt Col
Commanding 12 (W.S.Y.) Bn. S.L.I.

WAR DIARY or INTELLIGENCE SUMMARY

Army Form C. 2118.

12th (West Somerset Yeomanry) Bn. Som. L.I.

Place	Date	Hour	Summary of Events and Information	Remarks and references to Appendices
Sh. 36 S.W. M.36.b.5.W	October 1918			
	10		Billets at HERLIES. Bn HQ T4d 50. The Bde relieved the 23rd Bde in the line. At 1800 the Bn moved out to relieve the 2nd R.W.F. and the two left Coys K.S.L.I. Three Coys in the line in the order of A.B.D. Coys "B" Coy on right from O.34.b.8.2 to O.22.a.6.2. "C" Coy in Support at O.28.c.3.3. Bn. HQ O.26.d.6.1. "A" Coy. 4/12	
	11		Disposition of Bn "A" Coy O.34.b.8.2 to O.28.d.7.5.35. "B" Coy O.28d.25.35 to O.28.a.8.55. D Coy O.28.a.9.7 to O.22.a.6.1. "C" Coy in wood about O.28.c.33. Bn HQ O.26.d.6.1. LFEA Nil. Four blue and green SOS gas shells on O.29.a & c. Patrols reported enemy holding line of railway in O.29.t.8.d and O.23.a and c. Casualties 1 O.R. killed. Enemy artillery normal. M.G normal. M.G active.	
	12		Situation as for 11th. Enemy slightly normal. Three patrols went out during the night and one by day who reported enemy holding the line of railway in strength firing M.Gs. Found 11 Enemy dead. Casualties. 3 Lys. O.R. killed. 5 O.R. wounded. LFEA Nil. Cas Nil.	

Commanding 12th (W.S.Y.) Bn. S.L.I.

A. Moore Lt Col

Army Form C. 2118.

WAR DIARY
or
INTELLIGENCE SUMMARY

(Erase heading not required.) 12th (West Somerset Yeomanry) Bn Som. L.I.

Place	Date	Hour	Summary of Events and Information	Remarks and references to Appendices
UK Map FRANCE Sheet 36 S.W.	October 1918			
	13		Disposition as for 11th. Enemy artillery active also M.G.ª Four patrols went out by day and three by night, found enemy still holding line of railway in strength with M.G's forward. Casualties 3 OR wounded	
"	14		Disposition as for 11th. Enemy artillery & M.G. very active. Day patrol in touch with enemy on railway. 19.50 Relieved by the 14th R.H. and came into Support at PETIT HAUBOURDIN	
"	15		The enemy retired. 14th R.H. advanced and occupied the railway line. 14.00 Two Coys came under the command of O.C. 14th R.H. and took up defensive flank on left. Bn HQ 022 c 9.2.	
"	16		Defensive flank withdrawn + Bn in Support on railway A.E. coy on right, B&D coys on left. Bn HQ 022 c 9.2	
"	17		6.00 am Enemy retired. Marched from railway to HAUBOURDIN. 17.00 marched from HAUBOURDIN and billeted in	
d Sheet 36 S.E.			THUMESNIL	

G. Moore Lt Col
Commanding 12th (WSY) Bn S.L.I.

Army Form C. 2118.

WAR DIARY
or
INTELLIGENCE SUMMARY
(Erase heading not required.)

12th (West Somerset Yeomanry) Bn Som LI

Place	Date	Hour	Summary of Events and Information	Remarks and references to Appendices
Mob Ref Sheet 44. NSE 1/40000	18		October 1918	
			At 0800 marched from THUMESNIL to LEZENNES at 1000 ABLE Coy under Capt. T.A. RATTRAY took "Northern defensive flank" at 1900 defensive flank with own whole Bn billeted at ASCQ Bn HQ R16d 25.95	
	19		Bn H.Q. at ASCQ At 1500 marched through 16th Division and became advanced guard, 1st objective (line N⁰ 3 through N19 a 2 e central) At 1430 pushed on to 2nd objective road N⁰ 8 through N24 b N21 d d 6. N22 a N16 c) which was reached at 1900 and took up outpost line on road with forward posts. A Coy on right D Coy on left* Bn HQ N20 d 3.5 Casualties 1 O.R. wounded Lieut Hollis to hospital	
	20		0800 advanced on 1st objective (N23 d central, N23 a central, N29 b central) which was reached at 0900 at 1500 marched on second objective our line held up at 2nd and outpost line taken up at N18 central N24 to N30 d 9.9 Casualties Wounded 2 Lt W. WILLIAMS and 6. O.R. McLAUGHLAN	

AJ Cook
Lt Col.
Commanding 12th (W.Sy.) Bn S.L.I

WAR DIARY
or
INTELLIGENCE SUMMARY

(Erase heading not required.) 12th (West Somerset Yeomanry) Bn Som.L.I.

Army Form C. 2118.

Place	Date	Hour	Summary of Events and Information	Remarks and references to Appendices
Ref Map Sheet 37 SW 1/20000	October 1918			
	21		Line advanced until it ran O26e.22, O25d 5.5, O25c 8.5, O25a32, O19e82, O19central, O13d 29. At 21.10 after a short artillery barrage an advance was made to reach the road running from O27e.50 to O15c10.7. Considerable opposition was met with, very heavy MG and TM fire encountered and line was held up at O27c.14, O21a2.0, O15a3.0. Bn HQ O26a 7.4. OR.Q wounded & Lt H Wilde (late Yeth Y/h). Casualties killed 4. OR. wounded 32 & H. Wilde and 23. OR.	
	22		Line as for 21st A Coy from O27e.14 to O21e.1.1, B.Coy O21e.1.1 to O21a2.5 D Coy from O21a2.5 to O15a3.0. Bn HQ O26a7.4. At 21.00 the Bn was relieved by the 14th R.H. and came into billets in Support at OREQ. Casualties killed 2. OR wounded 14. OR.	
"	23		Bn in Support in billets at OREQ. At 15.00 "C" Coy was placed at the disposal of 14th R.H. in Support. Casualties OR wounded.	

E. A. [illegible] Lt Col.
Commanding 12th S.L.I.

Army Form C. 2118.

INTELLIGENCE SUMMARY.

(Erase heading not required.) 12th (West Somerset Yeomanry) Bn Som. L.I.

Place	Date	Hour	Summary of Events and Information	Remarks and references to Appendices
Ref Map Sheet 34 SW 1/50,000	October 1918			
	24		Bn in Bde Support in billets at ORCQ. At 1700 the Bn was relieved by the Sussex Bn, & 23th fifty Bath and marched to billets at CAMPHIN.	
	25		Billets at CAMPHIN. Parade under Coy Commanders for re-organisation and taking note of deficiencies.	
	26		Billets at CAMPHIN. Parades under Coy Commanders. Signalling, Scouts, Lewis Gun, and Stretcher Bearers instructional classes re-commenced.	
	27		Billets at CAMPHIN. Bn Church Parade at 1100.	
	28		Billets at CAMPHIN. Instructional Classes continued. Parades under Coy Commanders. 2nd Lt Ryland Howard reported to Bn. 3 St W.T. TOONE, 2 Lt E.G. SWINFORD joined the Bn from 2nd Bn S.L.I.	

E. M????
Lt Col.
Commanding 12th (W.S.Y) Bn S.L.I

HQ 229th Infty Bde

Herewith War Diary
for month of October.

R.T. Donnell Capt
1/11/18   Adj 12 S.L.I

WAR DIARY
or
INTELLIGENCE SUMMARY.

(Erase heading not required.) 12th (West Somerset Yeo) Bn Som. L.I.

Army Form C. 2118.

Place	Date	Hour	Summary of Events and Information	Remarks and references to Appendices
Ref Map Sheet 27.S.W 1/20,000	October 1918			
	29		Billets at CAMPHIN. Parades under Coy Commanders. Instructional classes continued. "B" Coy had use of 30 yds range. At 11.00 The Commanding Officer inspected "A" Coy in full marching order and "B" Coy at 11.00.	
	30		Billets at CAMPHIN. Parades under Coy Commanders & Instructional classes continued. Billeting arrangements of equipment etc. At 11.00 The Commanding Officer inspected "C" Coy in full marching order and "D" Coy at 11.00. The Divisional Band played selections from 15.00 to 17.00. Bn had use of baths from 13.00 to 19.00	
	31		Billets at CAMPHIN. Parades under Coy Commanders. Instructional classes continued. "C" Coy had use of 30 yds range. At 10.30 the Commanding Officer inspected HQ in full marching order and all transport at 10.30. Bn had use of baths from 10.500 to 13.00	

A. N. [signature]
Lt Col.
Commanding 12th S.L.I.

HQ 229th Infty Bde

Herewith WAR DIARY
for month of Novr.

2/12/18

R.T. Dommett Capt.
Adj. 12. S.L.I.

Army Form C. 2118.

WAR DIARY
or
INTELLIGENCE SUMMARY.
(Erase heading not required.) 12th (West Somerset Yeomanry) Bar. Som. L.I.

Place	Date	Hour	Summary of Events and Information	Remarks and references to Appendices
Rt. Mot FRANCE Sheet 37.	November 1918.			
	1.		Billets at CAMPHIN. Parade under Coy Commanders. Instructional classes continued. 1 NCO. and 3 men per platoon of A & B Coys had instruction in firing live rifle grenades under Lt. B.L. Haddon.	
	2.		Billets at CAMPHIN. The Bn was inspected by the B.G.C. in full marching order, commencing with the transport at 1000. After the inspection the Bn entered a demonstration in the use of the smoke grenade to blind a machine gun nest by one platoon of "A" Coy.	
	3.		Holy Communion at Bn HQ at 0800. The Bn moved to BAISIEUX for a Church Parade Service. Voluntary service at 1830.	
	4.		Billets at CAMPHIN. Parade under Coy Commanders. Instructional classes continued. 1 NCO and 3 men per platoon of C & D Coys received instruction in firing live rifle grenades under Lt. B.L. Haddon.	

J.S. Rattray Capt. for Lt. Col.
Commanding 12. S.L.I.

WAR DIARY
or
INTELLIGENCE SUMMARY.
(Erase heading not required.) 12th (West Somerset Yeo) Bn Som. L.I.

Army Form C. 2118.

Place	Date	Hour	Summary of Events and Information	Remarks and references to Appendices
Ref Map FRANCE. Sheet 37	November 1918			
	5		Billets at CAMPHIN. Parades under Coy Commanders. Instructional Classes continued. The Commanding Officer carried out a reconnaissance of the Bde area immediately South of Divisional boundry.	
	6		Billets at CAMPHIN. The G.O.C. inspected the Bn in Mass formation on the Bn alarm post at 0900. Parades under Coy Commanders.	
	7		Billets at CAMPHIN. Parades under Coy Commanders. Instructional classes continued.	
	8		Billets at CAMPHIN. Parades under Coy Commanders. Instructional classes continued.	
	9		Billets at CAMPHIN. Parades under Coy Commanders. Instructional classes continued.	
	10		Billets at CAMPHIN. at 0800 the Bn marched to HAVINNES via TOURNAI arriving at 1500 and went into billets.	

JSPotts Capt for Lt Col
Commanding. 12. S.L.I.

Army Form C. 2118.

WAR DIARY
or
INTELLIGENCE SUMMARY.
(Erase heading not required.) 1/2 (West Somerset Yeomanry) Bn Som L.I.

Place	Date	Hour	Summary of Events and Information	Remarks and references to Appendices
Ref Map FRANCE Sheet 34 1/100,000	November 1918. Sunday 11		Billets at HAVINNES. Marched at 0900 to en route for ESCALETTE. At 1045 when on road at L.25.c.1.95 news was received that an armistice had been signed by the enemy and that hostilities would cease at 1100. Men were made. The march was resumed at 1130 reaching ESCALETTE at 1700 and billeted.	
BELGIUM Sheet 38 1/100,000	12		Billets at ESCALETTE. Marched at 0900 en route for OLLIGNIES. Arriving at 1530 at billets, taking up an outpost line. C Coy on right supported by A Coy. B Coy on left supported by D Coy with post at J.7.b.2.1, J.1.c.5.0, J.1.b.1.5 & D.25.d.1.0. D.25.b.2.0. D19.d.3.3. Outpost line of resistance sited at J.7.b.1.9, J.1.b.3.0, J.1.a.0.6, D.25.d.7, D.25.d.5.5, D.25.d.4.7, D.25.d.3.9, D.25.b.1.1, D.25.a.9.7, D19.c.9.1, D19.d.0.7, D19.b.0.2.	
	13		Billets at OLLIGNIES. C & D Coys in outpost line, A & B Coys cleaning and repairing roads.	

J.S. Ratts Capt. for Lt Col.
Commanding 1/2. S.L.I.

Army Form C. 2118.

WAR DIARY
or
INTELLIGENCE SUMMARY.

(Erase heading not required.) 1/2nd (West Somerset Yeomanry) Bn. Som. L.I.

Instructions regarding War Diaries and Intelligence Summaries are contained in F.S. Regs., Part II, and the Staff Manual respectively. Title pages will be prepared in manuscript.

Place	Date	Hour	Summary of Events and Information	Remarks and references to Appendices
Ref. Map. BELGIUM Sheet 28.	November 1918.			
	14		Billets at OLLIGNIES. Disposition for Bde. Coy. as for 13th. Instructional Classes continued. Training under Coy Commdrs continued.	
	15		Billets at OLLIGNIES. Disposition for Bde. Coy as for 13th. Parades under Coy Commdrs. Instructional classes continued. "A" Coy road making.	
	16		Billets at OLLIGNIES. Disposition as for 13th. Instructional classes continued. Training under Company Commanders continued.	
	17		Billets at OLLIGNIES. The Bn. formed up in Mass formation on the Village Square at 0930, and at the invitation of the Burgomaster, Council and inhabitants took part in a procession to demonstrate the deliverance of BELGIUM from the oppressor of the enemy. At 1030 marched to MAIN VAULT arriving at 1530 and going into billets.	

J.S. Ratts Capt
Commanding 1/2 S.L.I.

Army Form C. 2118.

WAR DIARY
or
INTELLIGENCE SUMMARY

(Erase heading not required.) 12 (West Somerset Yeo) Bn. Som. L.I.

Instructions regarding War Diaries and Intelligence Summaries are contained in F. S. Regs., Part II. and the Staff Manual respectively. Title pages will be prepared in manuscript.

Place	Date	Hour	Summary of Events and Information	Remarks and references to Appendices
R/M of Sheet 38 BELGIUM Aqoo Sheet 37	November 1918			
	18		Marched from Manroult at 0945 to LEUZE (Sheet 37). Arriving at 1300 and going into billets.	
	19		Billets at LEUZE. 0730 to 1600. 22 Officers 365. OR at work on the LEUZE-TOURNAI railway	
	20		Billets at LEUZE. Band D Coy at work on railway. A&C Coy HQ and Transport had use of 55th Divl baths.	
	21		Billets at LEUZE. A&C Coy at work on LEUZE-TOURNAI railway. B&D Coy Ceremonial and Recreational games.	
	22		Draft of Lt. NEILSON and 22. O.R. joined the Bn from U.K. Billets at LEUZE. B&D Coy at work on LEUZE-TOURNAI railway. A&C Coy Ceremonial drill and Recreational games.	
	23		Billets at LEUZE. A&C Coy at work on LEUZE-TOURNAI railway. B Coy route march. D Coy Ceremonial drill.	
	24		Billets at LEUZE. A&off & 100 at work on railway, remainder. B. Church Parade.	

J.S.Ritter Capt
Commanding 12- S.L.I.

Army Form C. 2118.

WAR DIARY
or
INTELLIGENCE SUMMARY.
(Erase heading not required.) 12 (West Somerset Yeomanry) Bn Som L.I.

Place	Date	Hour	Summary of Events and Information	Remarks and references to Appendices
R.Q.M of BELGIUM Sheet 37 H.9700	25		Billets at LEUZE. A&C Coys at work on LEUZE-TOURNAI railway. B Coy close order and ceremonial drill. D Coy Route march. The C.O. inspected the reinforcements at 0900.	
	26		Billets at LEUZE. B&D Coys at work on the LEUZE TOURNAI railway. A&C Coys route march under the C.O.	
	27		Billets at LEUZE. A&C Coys at work on railway. B&D Coys close order and ceremonial drill. Guard mounting. The C.O. inspected the reinforcements in full marching order.	
	28		Billets at LEUZE. B&D Coys at work on railway. A Coy route march. "C" Coy close order drill.	
	29		Billets at LEUZE. A&C Coys at work on railway. B Coy route march. D Coy close order and ceremonial drill.	
	30		Billets at LEUZE. B&D Coys at work on railway. A&C Coys close order drill and recreational games.	

J.S. Ralts Capt
Commanding 12 S.L.I.

D.A.G. 3rd Echelon

Herewith War Diary
for month of Dec. 1918.

C.R.Heyward
Cmdg 12th Somerset L.I. Major

Filed
10-1-19

Army Form C. 2118.

WAR DIARY
or
INTELLIGENCE SUMMARY
(Erase heading not required.) 12 (West Somerset Yeomany) Bn. S.L.I.

Dec/18

9819

Place	Date	Hour	Summary of Events and Information	Remarks and references to Appendices
Map Ref. BELGIUM. Sheet 37 / Hoton			December 1918.	
	1		Billets at LEUZE. A&C Coys at work on railway. Remainder of Bn. Church Parade at 0930.	
"	2		Billets at LEUZE. B&D Coys at work on railway. A&C Coys Ceremonial drill and Recreational games	
"	3		Billets at LEUZE. A&C Coys at work on railway. B&D Coys Close order drill and Recreational games.	
"	4		Billets at LEUZE. Educational classes continued. B&D Coys at work on railway. A&C Coys Ceremonial drill and recreational games.	
"	5		Billets at LEUZE. Parades under Officers commanding Companies. Recreational games. Lt Col G.S. Poole D.S.O. resumed command of the Bn on the return of Brig Genl Thackery D.S.O. M.C. Major C.R. Hayward rejoined Bn from Senior officers course Cambrai. 2/Lt R. Featherstone 3 Wilts, reported for duty.	20h

G.S. Poole
Major for Lt Col
Commanding 12. S.L.I

Army Form C. 2118.

WAR DIARY
or
INTELLIGENCE SUMMARY

(Erase heading not required.) 12th/War Somerset Yeomanry) Som. L.I.

Place	Date	Hour	Summary of Events and Information	Remarks and references to Appendices
Ref. Map BELGIUM Sheet 37 1/40000	December 1918			
	6		Billets at LEUZE. A&C Coys at work on railway. Educational classes continued. B&D Coy Parades under Coy Commdrs for Ceremonial drill & Recreational training.	
"	7		Billets at LEUZE. On the occasion of the visit of His Majesty King George V to the III Corps on this date, the Division was drawn up along the LEUZE – TOURNAI road about Q.24.c&d. The Battalion being about Q.24.d.15.45, as he got out of his car to walk through the Division he was greeted with rousing cheers, as he passed the Battalion followed closely by his two sons, the Army Corps and Divisional Commanders. All ranks were very demonstrative in showing their loyalty to their Sovereign by removing their headress and raising tremendous cheers with great enthusiasm.	
"	8		Billets at LEUZE. The Battalion marched to Divine Service at the theatre at 11.00.	

E.M. Young Lt Col
Commanding 12th S.L.I.

WAR DIARY
INTELLIGENCE SUMMARY

12th (West Somerset Yeomanry) Bn Somerset L.I.

Army Form C. 2118.

Place	Date	Hour	Summary of Events and Information	Remarks and references to Appendices
Ref Map BELGIUM. Sheet 37 1/40,000	December 1918			
	9		Billets at LEUZE. B & D Coys at work on railway. A & C Coys at disposal of Coy Commdrs for ceremonial drill and recreational training.	
	10		Billets at LEUZE. A & C Coys & 509 Head Quarters at disposal of Coy Commdrs. B & D Coys at the work on Railway. Bn & Coy Regdlers arrived. Educational class continued.	
	11		For instruction Capt NEILSON proceeded to Army Reception Camp for duty with 76/WRTT & 13 ORs returned to it for demobilisation. Billets at LEUZE. B & D Coys & 509 Head Qrs at work on Railway. A & C Coys at disposal of Coy Commdrs. + ORs (Coalminers) proceeded to UK for demobilisation. Educational class continued & ORs proceeded Educational class continued. 11 ORs (Coalminers) + 2 Lt Nolan reported from Infantry Course.	
	12		Proceeded to UK for demobilisation Billets at LEUZE. B & D Coys & 509 Head Qrs at work on Railway A & C Coys at the disposal of Coy Commdrs.	
	13			

E.N.M. Gurney Major
12 "D" (Wo) Bn Somm L.I.

… 12 (West Somerset Yeo) Bn Somer L.I.

WAR DIARY
INTELLIGENCE SUMMARY

Army Form C. 2118.

Place	Date	Hour	Summary of Events and Information	Remarks and references to Appendices
MAP REF BELGIUM Sheet 39 1/40,000	December 1918			
	13 (cont)		12 S.R. (Coal miners) proceeded to UK for demobilisation. 2/Lt FERRIS detailed as Conducting Officer.	
	14		M.T. Coys at work on Railway. B.D Coy. paraded under officers commanding Coys for military & recreational training. Educational class continued. 2/Lt KERSLAKE proceeded to 21st Squadron R.A.F. for training in observation.	
	15		The Battn marched from LEUZE at 0800 to OSTICHES (Sheet 39) arriving at 1400 & going into Billets.	
	16		The Battn moved to GRAMMONT (Sheet 39) arriving there & going into Billets at 1430.	
	17		Billets at GRAMMONT. The bourgmestre were at the disposal of the Coy Commanders for cleaning billets & equipment.	
	18		Billets at GRAMMONT. Coys at the disposal of Coy Comdrs for general platoon drill.	
	19		Billets at GRAMMONT. Coys paraded under Coy Commanders for platoon & ceremonial drill.	

C.M.Symons Major
Commdg 12th Bn (W.S.) Bn Somer L.I.

Army Form C. 2118.

WAR DIARY
or
INTELLIGENCE SUMMARY.
(Erase heading not required.) 12th (Yeo) Bn Somt L.I.

Instructions regarding War Diaries and Intelligence Summaries are contained in F. S. Regs., Part II. and the Staff Manual respectively. Title pages will be prepared in manuscript.

Place	Date	Hour	Summary of Events and Information	Remarks and references to Appendices
Map Ref Sheet 30 Mucro	December 1918			
	20		Billets at GRAMMONT. Major C.R. Hayward assumed command of the battalion in the absence of Lt Col Poole D.S.O. granted 30 days leave to U.K. 0900-1200 Military training under Company Commanders. 1000-1200 Educational training. 1300-1600 Recreational training. Lecture by D.A.D.V.S. on skin diseases in animals.	
	21		Billets at GRAMMONT. Trained as on the 20th.	
	22		Billets at GRAMMONT. 0730 Church Parade Service. 1300-1600 Inter platoon football matches.	
	23		Billets at GRAMMONT. 0900-1000 Military training. 1000-1300 Educational training. 1300-1600 Inter platoon football matches.	
	24		Billets at GRAMMONT. Parade again the 23rd.	
	25		Billets at GRAMMONT. The G.O.C. has declared a general Holiday. He wished all ranks XXmas wishes & all ranks success & Field Punishment No 2.	

E.M. Hayward Major
Comdg 12th (Yeo) Bn Somt L.I.

Army Form C. 2118.

WAR DIARY
or
INTELLIGENCE SUMMARY.

(Erase heading not required.) 1/5 (W.Y.) Bn Somerset L.I.

*Instructions regarding War Diaries and Intelligence Summaries are contained in F. S. Regs., Part II. and the Staff Manual respectively. Title pages will be prepared in manuscript.

Place	Date	Hour	Summary of Events and Information	Remarks and references to Appendices
Nept Rly Shed So Yvo.o.o	1918		December 1918	
	25		8 O.Rs dispatched for demobilization	
		11.15	Parade Church of England Service	
		13.30	Battalion Dinner	
	26		Billets at GRAMMONT. No day's work & Holiday	
	27	10.00	Billets at GRAMMONT. 09.00 –	
		13.00	Educational Training. 13.00 Recreational Training	
	28		Billets at GRAMMONT. The B.C. has used 5 baths for GRAMMONT	
	29		Billets at GRAMMONT. 10.45 Church of England Parade Service. Lt (T/Capt) F EDBROOK M.C. arrived	
	30		Billets at GRAMMONT. 09.00 – 10.00 & 10.00 – 13.00 Educational Training. 13.00 Recreational Training or 30.5	
	31		Billets at GRAMMONT	

E.W. Young Major
1/5 (W.Y.) Bn Som L.I

Army Form C. 2118.

WAR DIARY
INTELLIGENCE SUMMARY.

(Erase heading not required.)

1/2 th (fo) Bn Somerset L.I

Place	Date	Hour	Summary of Events and Information	Remarks and references to Appendices
Nort Robin des Yuoroo	January 1919			
	1.		Billets at GRAMMONT. The O.C. Division allowed New Years day to be observed as a holiday throughout the Division. 4 O.Rs demobilised	
	2.		Billets at GRAMMONT 0900-1000 Military Training. 1000-1200 Educational Training. 1300 Recreational Training. Parade as on 2."	
	3.		Billets at GRAMMONT. Parade as on 2."	
	4.		Billets at GRAMMONT. 0900-1000 Military Training. Parades in each Company commence under Platoon Officers. 1000-1200 Educational Training. Qualified Teachers hold classes. Sunday & Zend classes together. 1300 Recreation	
	5.		Billets at GRAMMONT. Church of England Parade service 1030. Recreation	
	6.		Billets at GRAMMONT. 0900 Batt. Route March 1030 demobilising	
	7.		Billets at GRAMMONT. 1030 Presentation of medal ribbons by C.Whatmough. Major Comdg. 1/5 Som L.I.	

WAR DIARY
or
INTELLIGENCE SUMMARY

Army Form C. 2118.

12/5 (of) B" Somerset L.I.

Place	Date	Hour	Summary of Events and Information	Remarks and references to Appendices
Ref Map Sheet 30 1/40000	January 1919			
	7 (cont)		P.O.C. Division the Batt" with the remainder of the Brigade paraded in the Market Square GRAMMONT. The following of the Batt" were awarded the Military Medal	
			29469 H/Cpl G. ARTHURS Military Medal	
			53991 M. NORTH do	
			— Pte E. SNOOK to	
		12oo	Brigade Recreational training	
	8		Batt" at GRAMMONT 0900-1000 Military training under Company Commanders Educational training on the aft. E Recreational	
			Sgt PARKER reported from Hospital	
	9		Batt" at GRAMMONT. Parades as on the 8.	
	10		Batt" at GRAMMONT 0900-1000 Military training under Company Commanders Platoon Company Drill Educational Recreational training as on the 9th	

W. Haywood Major
Comdg 12th Somerset L.I.

Army Form C. 2118.

WAR DIARY
or
INTELLIGENCE SUMMARY. 12th (po) Bn Somerset L.I.
(Erase heading not required.)

Instructions regarding War Diaries and Intelligence Summaries are contained in F. S. Regs., Part II. and the Staff Manual respectively. Title pages will be prepared in manuscript.

Place	Date	Hour	Summary of Events and Information	Remarks and references to Appendices
Ref Map Sheet 30	1919			
1/40000	11		Billets at GRAMMONT. 0900-1000 Military Training under Company Commanders. Saluting & Ceremonial Drill. 1000-1200 Education Training continued. 1300 Recreational Training. Football, Cross Country Runs. 2Lt MOSELEY and 17 O.Rs sent to Demobilization Concentration Camp.	
	12		Billets at GRAMMONT. Church parade service. 1300 Recreational Training.	
	13		Billets at GRAMMONT. C & D Coys. Headq'rs. Bn. batted at the baths, GRAMMONT. 0930 A & B Bn. Hq were inspected by the remainder of the day. Coy week at the disposal of Coy Commanders.	
	14		Billets at GRAMMONT. A & B Coys & Transport batted at the baths, GRAMMONT. C & D Coys were inspected in the morning of the day was at the disposal of Coy Commanders	

W. Wedgwood Major
Comdg 12th (So) Bn Somst. L.I.

Army Form C. 2118.

WAR DIARY
or
INTELLIGENCE SUMMARY.

(Erase heading not required.) 125 (Ho) Bn Contact L.I

Instructions regarding War Diaries and Intelligence
Summaries are contained in F. S. Regs., Part II.
and the Staff Manual respectively. Title pages
will be prepared in manuscript.

Place	Date	Hour	Summary of Events and Information	Remarks and references to Appendices
Reg Hqs Belgium Sheet 30 1/40000	1919 15		Billets at GRAMMONT. The Boys went on a route march	
		1300	Educational Training	
	16		Bltts at GRAMMONT 0900-1000 Military Training 1000-1200 Platoon drill & Manual. Company training Elementary & Special classes Butts at Duck of Bath keeping 1300 Recreational training	
	17		Billets at GRAMMONT. 0900 to 1000 Military Training and Company Commanders Platoon drill, Manual 1000-1200 Educational Training, Elementary & Special classes Sinford French Book-keeping 1300 Recreational Training 2nd Lt E.R. Sigsfeld and 23 O.R. went Demobilised Camp.	

C Wargent Major
Commanding 19th Somt L.I.

Army Form C. 2118.

WAR DIARY
or
INTELLIGENCE SUMMARY.
(Erase heading not required.) 12 (West Somerset Yeo) Bn Som L.I.

Place	Date	Hour	Summary of Events and Information	Remarks and references to Appendices
Ref Map Belgium Sheet 30 1/40000	18		Billets at GRAMMONT. 0900 to 1000 Military Training under Company Commanders, Company Platoon and Section drill. 1000-1200 Educational Classes Elementary and Special, Shorthand, Book-keeping French and ... cold ...	
"	19	0830	Billets at GRAMMONT. Holy Communion at Parade Service at 1030	
"	20		Billets at GRAMMONT. 0900-1000 Parades under Company Commanders, to practice forming eighth	
		1000	The Bn formed up to practice the march past	
"	21		Billets at GRAMMONT. 0900-1100 Inspection of the Bn by the B.G.C. 231st Bde, transport at 1115.	
		1300	Recreational training	

C M Edwards Major
Commanding 12. S.L.I.

Army Form C. 2118.

WAR DIARY
or
INTELLIGENCE SUMMARY.
(Erase heading not required.)

1/2nd (West Somerset Yeo) Bn Som L.I.

Place	Date	Hour	Summary of Events and Information	Remarks and references to Appendices
Ref Map BELGIUM Sheet 30 1/40,000	January 1918			
	22		Billets at GRAMMONT. Parades under Company Commanders 0900 - 1100. Ceremonial drill, marching past, forming eights.	
	23		Billets at GRAMMONT. Commanding Officer inspected the Battn prior to departure for Brussels. B.G.C 231st Bde inspected Battn transport at 1500.	
	24		Billets at GRAMMONT. Battn Transport proceeded to Brussels at 08.00. 0915 B.G.C. 231st Bde held a final inspection at GRAMMONT of the Batts prior to proceeding to BRUSSELS	
	25		Billets at GRAMMONT. at 0745 the Bn embussed for BRUSSELS arriving at 1030 and going into billets at ANDERLECT.	

E.W. Hesse? Major
Commanding 12 Som L.I.

Army Form C. 2118.

WAR DIARY
or
INTELLIGENCE SUMMARY

(Erase heading not required.) 12th (West Somerset Yeomanry) Bn Som L.I.

Instructions regarding War Diaries and Intelligence Summaries are contained in F. S. Regs., Part II, and the Staff Manual respectively. Title pages will be prepared in manuscript.

Places	Date	Hour	Summary of Events and Information	Remarks and references to Appendices
Ref Map Belgium Sheet 30 1/40,000	January 1919			
	26		Billets at ANDERLECT. At 0930 the Bn formed up in column of Companies in the PLACE de WAYEZ, and joined the Composite Brigade Group from the 74th Division at starting point (Canal Bridge East end RUE WAYEZ), the Bn then moved to the BOULEVARD de WATERLOO and joined the procession of the III Corps, to be reviewed by and march past the King of the BELGIANS.	
	27		Billets at ANDERLECT. No parades. All ranks allowed to visit Brussels.	
	28		Billets at ANDERLECT. The Bn entrained for GRAMMONT at 1030 arriving about 1320.	
	29		Billets at GRAMMONT. Parades under Company Commanders. Educational & Recreational Training continued.	

E Udeyward Major.
Commanding 12th Som L.I.

Army Form C. 2118.

WAR DIARY
or
INTELLIGENCE SUMMARY.

(Erase heading not required.) 12th (West Somerset Yeo) Bn Som L I

Instructions regarding War Diaries and Intelligence Summaries are contained in F. S. Regs., Part II. and the Staff Manual respectively. Title pages will be prepared in manuscript.

Place	Date	Hour	Summary of Events and Information	Remarks and references to Appendices
Ref Map. BELGIUM. Sheet 30 1/40,000	January 1918.			
	30		Billets at GRAMMONT. Parades under Company Commanders. Educational & Recreational Training continued.	
	31		Billets at GRAMMONT. Bath Parade to nee of Divisional Baths at Civil Hospital all day ABCD Coys Bathing Capt R. T. Juersha M.C. Educational training continued 20 O.R's demobilized	

Lt Colonel and Major
Comdg 12th (Yeo) Bn Somerset L.I.

WAR DIARY or INTELLIGENCE SUMMARY.

12th (W. Sons. Yeo) Batt. Somerset L.I.

Place	Date	Hour	Summary of Events and Information	Remarks and references to Appendices
	February 1919.			
Billets at GRAMMONT.	1		Church parade service at 11.00. 26 O.R's demobilized.	
Billets at GRAMMONT.	2		Parades under Coy Commanders. Educational & Recreational training continued.	
Billets at GRAMMONT.	3		Parades under Coy Commanders. Educational & recreational training continued. 30 O.R's demobilized.	
Billets at GRAMMONT.	4		Parades under Company Commanders. Educational & recreational training continued. 21 O.R's to UK for demobilization.	
Billets at GRAMMONT.	5		Parades under Coy Cmdrs & usual Educational & recreational training continued. Draft to H.R. Fusrs & R. Hampshires.	
Billets at GRAMMONT.	6		Parades under Coy Cmdrs Educational & recreational training continued. 32 O.R's to UK for demobilization.	

J.P. Rattan MAJOR
O/Cdg 12 (W.S. Yeo) Batt. Somerset L.I.

Army Form C. 2118.

WAR DIARY
or
INTELLIGENCE SUMMARY.

(Erase heading not required.) 12th (W.S.Yeo) Bn Somerset L.I.

Place	Date	Hour	Summary of Events and Information	Remarks and references to Appendices
Ref Map			February 1919.	
Belgium Sheet 30	7		Billets at GRAMMONT. Parades under Coy Commanders. Educational & recreational training continued. 16 ORs demobilized.	
1/40000	8	10.45	Billets at GRAMMONT. Church Parade Service in St Josephs Hall at 10.45. Capt Rd F Shadow & 14 ORs proceeded to UK for demobilization.	
	9		Billets at GRAMMONT. Parades under Coy commanders. Educational & recreational training continued. 15 ORs to UK for demobilization.	
	10		Billets at GRAMMONT. Parades under Coy Commanders. Educational & recreational training continued.	
	11		Billets at GRAMMONT. Parades under Coy Commanders. Educational & recreational training & recreation continued.	

J.S.Ratts Major
Adjt 12th (W.S.Yeo) Bn Somerset L.I.

Army Form C. 2118.

WAR DIARY
or
INTELLIGENCE SUMMARY.

(Erase heading not required.) 12th (W.S. Yeo) Bn Somerset L.I.

Place	Date	Hour	Summary of Events and Information	Remarks and references to Appendices
Ref Map 12 Belgium Sheet 30 1/40000	February 1919			
	12		Billets at GRAMMONT. The Baths have the use of the Divn Baths but owing to bad weather no water could be obtained & consequently no clean clothing was available.	
	13		Billets at GRAMMONT. Parades under Coy Commanders. Lt. Col. C.R. Hayward proceeded to U.K. for demobilization & command of the Batln devolves upon Major T.A. RATTRAY M.C. 2/Lt. Tenterden proceeded to RE dispersing officers Tournai for duty.	
	14		Billets at GRAMMONT. Parades under Coy Commander. 40 ORs demobilized 2/Lt Richards conducting.	
	15		Billets at Grammont. Parades under Coy Commanders. 2 ORs demobilized. Sgt. B. Newman awarded D.C.M. (authy London Gazette 1.1.19)	
	16		Billets at GRAMMONT. Voluntary Holy Communion & service in Somersets' recreation room.	

J.F. Ratts Major
O.C. 12th (W.S. Yeo) Batln Somerset L.I.

Army Form C. 2118.

WAR DIARY
or
INTELLIGENCE SUMMARY.
(Erase heading not required.)

12th (N.S. Yeo) Bath Somerset L.I.

Instructions regarding War Diaries and Intelligence Summaries are contained in F. S. Regs., Part II, and the Staff Manual respectively. Title pages will be prepared in manuscript.

Place	Date	Hour	Summary of Events and Information	Remarks and references to Appendices
Ref. Map			February 1919.	
Belgium	17		Billets at GRAMMONT. Parades under Company Commander	
Sheet 30			5 OR's to demobilization Camp. Pte G.R. Hopgood to RAOC	
			Orders for duty	
1/40000	18		Billets at GRAMMONT. Parades under Coy Commander. Rifles & Lewis Guns were examined by Inspector of Armourers.	
	19		Billets at GRAMMONT. Parades under Coy Commander. 30 OR's & 1 Off'r to UK for demobilization	
	20		Billets at Grammont. Parades as on 19th. 5 OR's for demobilization	
	21		Billets at GRAMMONT. Parades under Coy Commander.	
	22		Billets at GRAMMONT. Parades under Coy Cmdr. 2 OR's demobilized	
	23		Billets at GRAMMONT. Church Parade service at 10.00. 4 OR's demobilized.	
	24		Billets at GRAMMONT. Parades under Coy Commander.	

J.S. Ritter
Major
Cmdg (12th Yeo Bn) Somerset L.I.

Army Form C. 2118.

WAR DIARY
or
INTELLIGENCE SUMMARY

2nd (W.S. Yeo) Batt. Somerset L.I.

Place	Date	Hour	Summary of Events and Information	Remarks and references to Appendices
Nr. Hqrs. Belgium	25		Billets at GRAMMONT. Parades under Coy Commanders. Lecture by Capt K.C. PONSONBY on "Little Staffs of the war in Palestine"	
Staff	26		Billets at GRAMMONT. Parades under Coy Comdrs. Bath.	
1/400-0			Parade at 11.00 am Recreation room. 1 OR Lewis Light.	
	27		Billets at GRAMMONT. Parades under Coy Commanders.	
	28		Billets at GRAMMONT. Parades under Coy Commanders. Elementary education from this day under Batt. arrangements. 2 ORs to U.K. for demobilization. Up to date 40 ORs have re-enlisted in Regular Army.	

J.S. Ratts
Major
Cmdg 12th (W.S. Yeo) Batt. Somerset L.I.

HQ 229th Infty Bde.

Herewith War Diary for month of March please.

R.T. Donnett. Capt.
31-3-19 & O.C. 13th Somerset L.I.

WAR DIARY
or
INTELLIGENCE SUMMARY
(Erase heading not required.) 12TH (N. Som. Yeo.) Battn. Somerset L.I.

Army Form C. 2118.
MARCH 1919

Vol 12

Place	Date	Hour	Summary of Events and Information	Remarks and references to Appendices
Ref Map			March 1919	
Belgium Sheet 30	1st		Billets at GRAMMONT. Parties under Coy Commanders. ft	
			L.G.C. March to UK to demobilisation. Summer time came	
			into force on this date.	
1/40000	2		Billets at GRAMMONT. Church Parade service in 14 R.S.	
			Recreation room at 1000.	
	3		Billets at GRAMMONT. Parades under Coy Commanders.	
	4		Billets at GRAMMONT. Parades under Coy Commanders.	
	5		Billets at GRAMMONT. 5 officers & 158 O.R.s despatched this	
			day to 3/4 Bns & Bucks L.I. for Army of Occupation.	
	7		Billets at GRAMMONT. Parades under Capt J.H. Fairthful.	
			C.O. & Howarer MAJOR I.A. RATTRAY M.C. wearing rank of Lt.Col. leaving	
			Attached from G.H.Q. & Lieut E.F. HOBBS wearing rank of Captain	
	8		Billets at GRAMMONT. Parades under Captain J.H. Fairthful	
			Lieut Col C.S. Poole D.S.O. relinquished rank of Lt-Col & reverts to substantive	
			rank of Major (19.1.19)	

J.A. Potts
LIEUT-COL
CMDG 12TH (YEO) Battn. Somerset L.I.

23m

WAR DIARY
or
INTELLIGENCE SUMMARY.

Army Form C. 2118.

12th (W. Som Yeo) Somerset L.I.

Place	Date	Hour	Summary of Events and Information	Remarks and references to Appendices
	March 1919			
Grammont	8		Billets at GRAMMONT. Church parade under Capt. G.H. Fairfyfe	
Grammont	9		Billets at GRAMMONT. Church of England parade service at 10.0.0.	
Ninove	10		Billets at GRAMMONT. Parade under Brig. G. Fairfyfe	
Grammont	11		Billets at GRAMMONT. Parade under Capt. G. Fairfyfe. 27 ORs	
			to UK to demobilization	
	12		Billets at GRAMMONT. Parades under Capt. D. Cross D.C.M.	
			Capt G.H. Fairfyfe to UK to rejoin regular unit.	
	13		Billets at GRAMMONT. Parades under Capt. D. Cross D.C.M.	
			Parades 20 on 14th 13th	
	14		Billets at GRAMMONT. Parades under Capt. D. Cross D.C.M.	
	15		Billets at GRAMMONT. Parades no on 14th 23 ORs to demobilisation.	
	16		Billets at GRAMMONT. Church of England parade service at 10.0.0.	
	17		Billets at GRAMMONT. Parades under Capt. D. Cross D.C.M.	
			Trooper (W.Som Yeo) Owen killed in Potzgilby Cross Country London Ongot 1/1 - 2/4	
			Nos. 1 & 2 Platoons relinquished here strength & went to Lieutenant 22.12.18	

J.B.Ratts Lt. Col.

Cdg. (12 Bn) Somerset L.I.

WAR DIARY
or
INTELLIGENCE-SUMMARY.

(Erase heading not required.)

Army Form C. 2118.

12th (N. Ser. Bn.) Somerset L.I.

Place	Date	Hour	Summary of Events and Information	Remarks and references to Appendices
			March 1919	
Field N⁰ 18	18		Billets at GRAMMONT. Parades under Capt A.C. Cross D.C.M.	
Belgium	19		Billets at GRAMMONT. Parades as on 18th.	
Sheet 30	20		Billets at GRAMMONT. Parades of P.W. Force in fatigues.	
1/40000	21		Billets at GRAMMONT. Parades under Capt W.C. Cross D.C.M. Hunt	
			P.K. Halliwell & 11 O.R's to UK for Demobilization	
	22		Billets at GRAMMONT. Bath. Whist at Own Ratos.	
	23		Billets at GRAMMONT. Voluntary Church of England Service	
	24		Billets at GRAMMONT. The Bath changed Billets.	
	25		Billets at GRAMMONT. Parades under Capt W.C. Cross D.C.M.	
			2 of R's to UK for demobilization	
	26		Billets at GRAMMONT. Parades under Capt W.C. Cross D.C.M.	
	27		Billets at GRAMMONT. Parades under Capt W.C. Cross D.C.M.	
	28		Billets at GRAMMONT. Parades under Capt W.C. Cross D.C.M.	
			Battalion had use of the Baths.	
	29		Billets at Grammont. Parades under Capt W.C. Cross D.C.M.	
	30		Battalion had use of Foden Disinfector. Capt Houlding	
			and Lt A.G. Irwin to UK for Demobilization. J S Ratts Lt-Col.	
			Commanding 10th Somerset L.I.	

Army Form C. 2118.

WAR DIARY
or
INTELLIGENCE SUMMARY

(Erase heading not required.) 12th (West Somerset Yeo) Bn Somerset L.I.

Place	Date	Hour	Summary of Events and Information	Remarks and references to Appendices
Map Ref. BELGIUM	March 1919			
Sheet-30	30		Billets at GRAMMONT. Inspection by the Commanding Officer.	
/4000	31		Billets at GRAMMONT. Parades small. Capt W.C. Cross Dem. Lieut. R.W. Ryatt, Lieut. Hopgood Dem. KERSLAKE and 1 O.R. to UK for demobilization.	

J.O. Patton
Lt Col
Commanding 12th Somerset L.I.

HQ 229th Infty Bde.

Herewith War Diary for month of April please.

R.H. Dommett. Capt
Adj 12th Somerset. L.I.

1-5-19.

Army Form C. 2118.

WAR DIARY
or
INTELLIGENCE SUMMARY.

(Erase heading not required.) 12th (West Somerset) Bn. SOMERSET. L.I.

No 13

Place	Date	Hour	Summary of Events and Information	Remarks and references to Appendices
Ref Map BELGIUM. Sheet 30 1/40000	April 1.		Billets at GRAMMONT. Physical and Recreational Training.	
	2.		Billets at GRAMMONT. Physical and Recreational Training.	
	3.		Billets at GRAMMONT. Physical and Recreational Training.	
	4.		Billets at GRAMMONT. Physical and Recreational Training. Lt. B. H. H. BROWN, 2Lt E.R. Cowan & 1OR to UK for demobilization. Lt. G.A. RATTRAY M.C. having proceeded to UK on leave, the command of the Bn. devolves on Capt. W. C. CROSS, D.C.M.	
	5.		Billets at GRAMMONT. Parade for Divine Service under the Commanding Officer at 10.50. 295004 C.S.M. BELLAMY. I. H. } Awarded Meritorious 295124 C.Q.M.S. BIFFIN. A.J. } Service Medal. 295219 Sergt. BLACKMORE. C. } London Gazette d/18.1.19.	
	6.		Billets at GRAMMONT. Physical and Recreational Training	
	7.		Billets at GRAMMONT. Physical and Recreational Training Pte. J.H. CASEY. Attacked R.T.D. at ENGHIEN. Two OR to Hospital.	
	8.		Billets at GRAMMONT. Physical and Recreational Training. R.J.D. Ommanetty Capt. Commanding 12th Somerset. L. I.	24m

Army Form C. 2118.

WAR DIARY
or
INTELLIGENCE SUMMARY.

(Erase heading not required.) 12th (West Somerset Yeo) Bn. Somerset L.I.

Instructions regarding War Diaries and Intelligence Summaries are contained in F. S. Regs., Part II. and the Staff Manual respectively. Title pages will be prepared in manuscript.

Place	Date	Hour	Summary of Events and Information	Remarks and references to Appendices
MAR REF BELGIUM. Sheet 30 40/30	April 9		Billets at GRAMMONT. Physical and Recreational Training.	
	10		Billets at GRAMMONT. Physical and Recreational Training. Six O.R. to R.A.O.C. One O.R. to Chinese Labour Corps.	
	11		Billets at GRAMMONT. Physical and Recreational Training. Capt. W.C. Cross. D.C.M. To U.K. for demobilisation. The Command of the Bn. devolves upon Capt. E.F. Hobbs.	
	12		Billets at GRAMMONT. Physical and Recreational Training.	
	13		Billets at GRAMMONT. Physical and Recreational Training.	
	14		Billets at GRAMMONT. Physical and Recreational Training. One O.R. to U.K. for demobilisation.	
	15		Billets at GRAMMONT. Physical and Recreational Training.	
	16		Billets at GRAMMONT. Physical and Recreational Training.	
	17		Billets at GRAMMONT. Physical and Recreational Training.	
	18		Billets at GRAMMONT. Physical and Recreational Training. 15 O.R. to 2/4 Oxford & Bucks. L.I. for Army of Occupation.	
	19		Billets at GRAMMONT. Physical and Recreational Training.	

R.J. Donnett. Capt.
Commanding 12th Somerset. L.I.

Army Form C. 2118.

WAR DIARY
or
INTELLIGENCE SUMMARY.

(Erase heading not required.) 12th (West Somerset (Yeo) Bn. SOMERSET. L.I.

Place	Date	Hour	Summary of Events and Information	Remarks and references to Appendices
Ref Map. BELGIUM Sheet 30	April			
	20		Billets at GRAMMONT. Physical and Recreational Training	
	21		Billets at GRAMMONT. Physical and Recreational Training. 38. OR reported to 11th Bn. S.L.I.	
	22		Billets at GRAMMONT. Physical and Recreational Training	
	23		Billets at GRAMMONT. Physical and Recreational Training	
	24		Billets at GRAMMONT. Physical and Recreational Training	
	25		Billets at GRAMMONT. Physical and Recreational Training	
	26		Billets at GRAMMONT. Physical and Recreational Training. Capt. E.F. HOBBS proceeded to U.K. for leave. The Command of the Bn devolves upon Capt. R.T. Donnett. Two Z mules to 59th M.V.S. Three X mules to COSCO. O. This closes the Bn animal a/c	
	27		Billets at GRAMMONT. Physical and Recreational Training	
	28		Billets at GRAMMONT. Physical and Recreational Training	
	29		Billets at GRAMMONT. Physical and Recreational Training	
	30		Billets at GRAMMONT. Physical and Recreational Training. 2/Lt W. WHITE, TOONE & FEATHERSTONE to 219. P.O.W. Coy.	

R.T. Donnett. Capt.
Commanding. 12th Somerset. L.I.

Army Form C. 2118.

WAR DIARY
or
INTELLIGENCE SUMMARY
(Erase heading not required.) 12th (West Somerset Yeo) Bn Somerset L.I.

9/8/14

Place	Date	Hour	Summary of Events and Information	Remarks and references to Appendices
At Mob. BELGIUM Lat 530 Long 3000	May 1919.			25th
	1.		Billets at Grammont. Physical and Recreational Training	
	2.		Billets at Grammont. Physical and Recreational Training	
			2/Lt Toone White & Featherstone to 319 P of W. Coy	
			Lt Col T.A. Rattray, M.C. having returned from leave, assumed command of Bn.	
	3.		Billets at GRAMMONT. Physical and Recreational Training	
	4.		Billets at GRAMMONT. Physical and Recreational Training	
	5.		Billets at GRAMMONT. Physical and Recreational Training	
	6.		Billets at GRAMMONT. Physical and Recreational Training	
	7.		Billets at GRAMMONT. Physical and Recreational Training	
	8.		Billets at GRAMMONT. Physical and Recreational Training	
	9.		Billets at GRAMMONT. Physical and Recreational Training	
	10.		Billets at GRAMMONT. Physical and Recreational Training	
			9. O.R. to UK for Demobilisation on reduction of Bn to Cadre Establishment	
	11.		Billets at GRAMMONT. Physical and Recreational Training	
	12.		Billets at GRAMMONT. Physical and Recreational Training	
	13.		Billets at GRAMMONT. Physical and Recreational Training	

J.D. Rattray Lt Col.
Commanding 12th Somerset L.I.

Army Form C. 2118.

WAR DIARY
or
INTELLIGENCE SUMMARY

(Erase heading not required.) 1/2 E (West Somerset Yeo) Bn Somerset L.I.

Instructions regarding War Diaries and Intelligence Summaries are contained in F. S. Regs., Part II. and the Staff Manual respectively. Title pages will be prepared in manuscript.

Place	Date	Hour	Summary of Events and Information	Remarks and references to Appendices
Nr Maf. BELGIUM Sheet 30 1/40000		May 1919		
	14		Billets at GRAMMONT. Physical and Recreational Training	
	15		Billets at GRAMMONT. Physical and Recreational Training. Capt E.F. HOBBS from leave	
	16		Billets at GRAMMONT. Physical and Recreational Training	
	17		Billets at GRAMMONT. Physical and Recreational Training	
	18		Billets at GRAMMONT. Physical and Recreational Training	
	19		Billets at GRAMMONT. Physical and Recreational Training	
			2Lt F.C. MATEER to No. 15 Ordnance Depot.	
	20		Billets at GRAMMONT. Physical and Recreational Training	
	21		Billets at GRAMMONT. Physical and Recreational Training	
	22		Billets at GRAMMONT. Physical and Recreational Training	
	23		Billets at GRAMMONT. Physical and Recreational Training	
	24		Billets at GRAMMONT. Physical and Recreational Training	
	25		Billets at GRAMMONT. Physical and Recreational Training	
	26		Billets at GRAMMONT. Physical and Recreational Training	

J.D. Rattray Lt Col.
Commanding 1/2 Somerset L.I.

Army Form C. 2118.

WAR DIARY
or
INTELLIGENCE SUMMARY.

(Erase heading not required.) 12th (West Somerset (Yeo) Bn Somerset L.I.

Place	Date	Hour	Summary of Events and Information	Remarks and references to Appendices
Ref Map. BELGIUM Sheet 30 1/40,000	May 1919			
	27.		Billets at GRAMMONT. Physical and Recreational Training	
	28.		Billets at GRAMMONT. Physical and Recreational Training.	
	29.		Billets at GRAMMONT. Physical and Recreational Training.	
	30.		Billets at GRAMMONT. Physical and Recreational Training	
			2/Lts Casey and Duncan to R.T.O. ENGHIEN and R.A.O.C. respectively and struck off strength of Bn from 16.5.19	
	31		Billets at GRAMMONT. Physical and Recreational Training	

J.S. Rattson
Lt. Col.
Commanding 12th Somerset L.I.

Army Form C. 2118.

WAR DIARY
or
INTELLIGENCE SUMMARY.
(Erase heading not required.) 1/2 (West Somerset Yeo) Bn Som.L.I.

Instructions regarding War Diaries and Intelligence Summaries are contained in F. S. Regs., Part II, and the Staff Manual respectively. Title pages will be prepared in manuscript.

Place	Date	Hour	Summary of Events and Information	Remarks and references to Appendices
Ref Map 51/U-30 Belgium 1/40000	France			
	1		Billets at GRAMMONT. Physical and Recreational training	
	2		Billets at GRAMMONT. Physical and Recreational training	
	3		Billets at GRAMMONT. Physical and Recreational training	
	4		2/Lt to UK for demobilisation.	
	5		Billets at GRAMMONT. Physical and Recreational training	
	6		Billets at GRAMMONT. Physical and Recreational training	
	7		2Lt G. RICHARDS to UK as conducting officer	
	8		Billets at GRAMMONT. Physical and Recreational training	
	9		Billets at GRAMMONT. Physical and Recreational training	
	10		Billets at GRAMMONT. Physical and Recreational training	
	11		Billets at GRAMMONT. Physical and Recreational training	
	12		Billets at GRAMMONT. Physical and Recreational training	
	13		Billets at GRAMMONT. Physical and Recreational training	
	14		Billets at GRAMMONT. Physical and Recreational training	
	15		Billets at GRAMMONT. Physical and Recreational training	

J.D. Rattle Lt Col
Commandant 1/2th Som.L.I.

Army Form C. 2118.

WAR DIARY
or
INTELLIGENCE SUMMARY.

(Erase heading not required.) 12TH (W.Som. Yeo) Bn Somerset L.I.

9 & 15

Place	Date	Hour	Summary of Events and Information	Remarks and references to Appendices
Sheet 30 1/40000	16		Billets at Grammont.	
	17		T.A. RATTRAY M.C. Capt E.F. HOBBS & 18 O.R's. embarked at Station Square GRAMMONT for GHISLENHEIN at 02.30. Entrained at 0615 arriving at 5TH ARMY DEMOBILIZATION CAMP, LILLE at 1300	
			The Bn Cadre consisting of Lieut-Col	
	18.		5TH ARMY DEMOBILIZATION CAMP LILLE. The Cadre paraded at 0700 entraining for BOULOGNE at 0800 at ST ANDRE STATION LILLE, arriving at BOULOGNE at 1400.	
	19		DEMOBILIZATION CAMP BOULOGNE The Cadre never camps to await embarkation for DOVER.	
	20.		DEMOBILIZATION CAMP BOULOGNE Embarked for UK at 1200 BOULOGNE	

J.S. Rattray
Cmdg 12TH (Yeo) Bn Somerset L.I.

26m

www.ingramcontent.com/pod-product-compliance
Lightning Source LLC
Chambersburg PA
CBHW081439160426
43193CB00013B/2324